THE ATLAS OF
ENDANGERED
ANIMALS

THE ATLAS OF
ENDANGERED
ANIMALS

WILDLIFE UNDER THREAT AROUND THE WORLD

PAULA HAMMOND

Marshall Cavendish
Reference

NEW YORK

This edition first published in 2010 in the United States of America by Marshall Cavendish.

Marshall Cavendish
99 White Plains Road
Tarrytown, New York 10591-9001

www.marshallcavendish.us

Library of Congress Cataloging-in-Publication Data

Hammond, Paula.
  The atlas of endangered animals : wildlife under threat around the world / Paula
Hammond.
     p. cm.
  Includes index.
  ISBN 978-0-7614-7872-0
  1. Endangered species. 2. Endangered species--Geographical distribution. I. Title.
  QL82.H34 2010
  591.68--dc22

                                    2008044956

Printed in China

13   12   11   10   09   1   2   3   4   5

Editorial and design by
Amber Books Ltd
Bradley's Close
74–77 White Lion Street
London N1 9PF
United Kingdom
www.amberbooks.co.uk

Project Editor: Sarah Uttridge
Design: Joe Conneally
Picture Research: Terry Forshaw

Artwork credits
All artworks © International Masters Publishers Ltd except for the following:
Amber Books: 38-39, 41, 116-117, 119
De Agostini: 44 (right), 45 (bottom left), 45 (bottom right)
Magic Group: 40 (bottom left), 118 (top left)
Marshall Cavendish: 42-43, 44 (left)

Picture credits
11: Jurgen & Christine Sohns/FLPA; 14: RF Gold; 18: ZSSD/Minden Pictures/FLPA; 23:
Photos.com; 26: Franz Lanting/Minden Pictures/FLPA;
34: Backgrounds Archive; 42: Gerry Ellis/Minden Pictures/FLPA;
57: Backgrounds Archive; 60: Jurgen & Christine Sohns/FLPA; 65: Photos.com; 68:
Photos.com; 80: U.S. Fish & Wildlife Services; 86: Konrad Wothe/Minden Pictures/FLPA;
90: Jurgen & Christine Sohns/FLPA; 94: Geoff Moon/FLPA; 106: Foto Natura
Stock/FLPA; 120: U.S. Fish & Wildlife Services; 132: Foto Natura Catalogue/FLPA; 151:
Fritz Polking/FLPA; 158: Backgrounds Archive; 162: Tui de Roy/Minden Pictures/FLPA;
176: Malcolm Schuyl/FLPA;
192: Photos.com; 199: NOAA Photo Library; 202: Foto Natura Catalogue/FLPA; 207:
Mike Parry/Minden Pictures/FLPA; 210: NOAA Picture Library;
214: NOAA Picture Library; 219: U.S. Fish & Wildlife Services

Contents

Introduction

Golden lion
tamarin

Nature is in danger. Worldwide, a total
of 733 animal species (mostly insects) are
thought to have become extinct in 2004. A further
7180 were listed as being 'Critically Endangered',
'Endangered' or 'Vulnerable'. This included 1101
mammals, 1213 birds and 304 reptiles. The roll call
of those at risk – compiled by the International
Union for the Conservation of Nature (IUCN)
– is surprisingly broad. The great white shark is
a fearsome predator which has been so
successful as a species that sharks as a group
have sat at the top of the food chain for 400
million years. Yet it appears on the IUCN's 'Red
List' of threatened species alongside that gentle
herbivore the giant panda. Many scientists believe
the current situation to be so serious that it can
be classed as a 'mass extinction event'.

Giant panda

North American salamander

Numbat

Giant otter

Desert tortoise

Mass extinctions are nothing new. They happen with surprising regularity. We know that at least five have occurred in our planet's history. This includes the one that wiped out the dinosaurs some 65 million years ago. What these past extinctions had in common was that they were the result of catastrophic natural disasters. Today, it is what we are doing that is proving to be every bit as destructive as Mother Nature: hunting, trading in animal products, introducing species from one region to another, and destroying natural habitats. Species are now dying out at a rate up to 1000 times faster than before the arrival of *Homo sapiens* – human beings. Now the continued survival of the endangered animals featured in this volume depends on the help and support of the very species that has done them the most harm – us.

Cassowary

Bengal tiger

EUROPE

Atlas Mountains

MEDITERRANEAN SEA

Libyan
Desert

Nile

Nubian
Desert

ARABIAN
SEA

S a h a r a

AFRICA

SOUTH ATLANTIC
OCEAN

Congo
Basin

Rift Valley

Lake
Victoria

Lake
Tanganyika

Lake
Nyasa

INDIAN
OCEAN

Namib Desert

Kalahari
Desert

MADAGASCAR

Cape of Good Hope

Africa

Africa is a continent of spectacular natural beauty: a vast landmass
that encompasses rolling, green grasslands and golden beaches,
rain-soaked tropical forests and parched desert sands.

This vast continent – the second largest – covers around one-fifth of the world's entire landmass, and about 75 per cent of it is virtually uninhabited. However, Africa's population is booming, and deforestation and industrialization present a real threat to the continent's wild, natural beauty. Already pollution, overfishing and the introduction of non-native fish species have wiped out half of Lake Victoria's 500 native species. African rainforests are vanishing at an alarming rate of around 142,450 square kilometres (55,000 square miles) a year. And in the Sahel – a strip of grassland dividing the mighty Sahara Desert in the north from the wetlands in the south – a vast amount of intensive farming is slowly but surely turning the region into an arid wasteland.

In 2004 alone, more animals became extinct in Africa than in all of the other continents put together.

Such environmental concerns are not unique to Africa. Unfortunately, though, Africa has many other problems to face. It contains many of the world's poorest countries, and war and famine are commonplace. Conservation, understandably, is not always the first priority. Despite such problems, however, Africa continues to create laws to protect its wildlife. All across the continent, countries are cooperating to create huge animal sanctuaries, such as the Serengeti National Park in Tanzania, which stretches all the way to the Masai Mara Reserve in Kenya, some 193 kilometres (120 miles) away. Such nature reserves represent a ray of hope for the continent's dying species.

Addax

The spiral-horned addax used to be one of nature's great success stories. In an environment where little else lived, this hardy desert dweller not only survived, but also thrived. Human hunters have now driven addax population numbers to a critical low, however, and unfortunately the future looks increasingly uncertain for this appealing and attractive antelope.

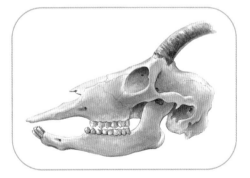

Skull

The addax's tough skull is designed to absorb the shock of impact when fully grown males head-butt each other during fights for dominance and mating rights.

Key Facts

ORDER *Artiodactyla* / FAMILY *Bovidae* / GENUS & SPECIES *Addax nasomaculatus*

Weight	60–125kg (132–276lb)
Length Head and body Tail	 1.5–1.7m (5ft–5ft 7in) 25–35cm (10–14in)
Shoulder height	95–110cm (3ft–3ft 7in)
Sexual maturity	2–3 years
Breeding season	Peaks in hottest and coldest months
Gestation period	257–264 days
Number of young	1
Birth interval	1 year
Typical diet	Desert grasses and shrub foliage
Life span	6–8 years

Coat

White reflects the sun, so the addax's almost white summer coat helps to keep this amazing antelope cool, even in the harshest of climates.

The addax is a heavily built member of the Family Bovidae, an animal group that includes wild cattle and goats. Built for stamina and endurance, rather than speed and agility, this is a tough desert nomad, designed for a life of extremes.

Living on the Edge

Despite popular perceptions, deserts are not all sand and cacti. Only 20 per cent of most deserts is covered by sand. The rest of the terrain is generally boulder-strewn scrubland, where grasses and low-lying bushes struggle to squeeze enough nutrients from the dry soil to grow. Temperatures can be extreme in these unforgiving landscapes. In the heat of the midday sun, temperatures can reach a scorching 48°C (118°F). At night, they can plummet to around 13°C (55°F) and sometimes close to freezing. Add regular high winds and sandstorms, and it is easy to see why the desert is so sparsely populated. When it does rain, though, a remarkable transformation takes place. For a few short weeks – as long as the rains last – the desert turns into a lush green paradise, as plants race to grow, flower and reproduce before the drought comes again. In such an extreme and changeable environment, it is no surprise that the addax is one of the few large mammals who have been able to make a living in these regions.

Addax habitat

Early Risers

As vegetation is sparse in the desert, the addax is forced to travel vast distances in search of a meal. To conserve energy, and to avoid moisture loss and dehydration, this tough antelope has adapted its lifestyle in order to stay as stay as cool as possible.

Comparisons

If there is any hope for the addax, this can be found in the story of its closest living relative, the larger scimitar-horned oryx (*Oryx dammah*). Once plentiful, the oryx is now extinct in the wild; however, captive breeding programmes have recently reintroduced oryx into Tunisia, and there is real hope that numbers in the wild will soon begin to recover. Similar programmes in Libya, Morocco and Tunisia may soon provide a similar lifeline to the struggling addax.

Addax

Scimitar-horned oryx

During the day, the addax tends to shelter from the heat of the sun. It is at its most active during the cooler hours before dawn, and when night falls. Surprisingly, for an animal that lives in one of the world's hottest and driest regions, the addax rarely drinks. Instead, it is able to get as much moisture as it needs from the plants and shrubs it eats. This is another reason for the addax to be an early riser, for this is the time when most plants will have a thin covering of dew, which provides a valuable extra source of liquid.

Threats and Conservation

Until the 1880s, herds of addax could be found from the deserts of North Africa to the Atlantic coastline. Such herds – headed by an older, dominant male – could be up to 50 strong, and occasionally formed into super-herds of 1000 or more individuals. Today it is unusual to see a herd of more than five animals.

A report from the IUCN in 1969 gives us some clue as to the sudden change in the addax's fortunes: 'All game was looked upon as a free source of meat and skins, and any animal – irrespective of sex or condition – [was] ruthlessly killed.' Put simply, generations of overhunting have brought the addax to the brink of extinction. It is a sad testament to humanity's destructive nature that the only areas where viable populations now survive are in uninhabited regions of Mauritania and the Western Sahara, and fenced reserves where captive breeding programmes are under way.

To keep their newborn calf safe from aggressive males, addax mothers leave the herd just before they are due to give birth.

After around six weeks, the new calf and his mother rejoin the herd, ready to start their long trek in search of food.

Being born in the rainy season, the calf's first trek will take place when the temperature is cooler and food more plentiful.

The calf has to be tough to survive in an environment where it will face freezing nights, scorching days and furious sandstorms.

African Elephant

From parched savannah scrublands to lush, forested mountain slopes, the elephant was once one of the most familiar sights in Africa's dramatic landscape. Yet, for decades, these truly awe-inspiring mammals have been hunted in huge numbers, with a devastating effect on populations throughout the continent.

Key Facts	ORDER *Proboscidea* FAMILY *Elephantidae* GENUS & SPECIES *Loxodonta africana*
Weight	Male up to 6000kg (6.7 tonnes); female smaller
Length	Male up to 4.5m (14.5ft), head to rump; female up to 3.3m (10ft 9in)
Shoulder height	Male up to 3.8m (12ft 8in); female about 2.7m (8ft 10in)
Sexual maturity	Female 10 years, male 15–18 years
Breeding season	All year
Gestation period	22 months
Number of young	1
Birth interval	3–4 years
Typical diet	Grasses, foliage, shrubs, fruit, flowers, roots
Life span	50–60 years

Eye glands

Every year, for about three months, glands beside an adult bull elephant's eye and ear become active. During this time, the mature males enter a condition called 'musth', which means madness.

Trunk

The elephant's trunk is a highly flexible prehensile gripping tool; it is useful for all sorts of tasks from handling food to caressing other members of the troop and carrying objects.

It has been 50 million years since the ancestors of the elephant first set foot on the Earth. Today, the mighty African elephant is one of the few remaining survivors of an ancient animal order (Proboscidea) that over time has boasted 350 species. Numbers may be declining, but as long as they survive, we have living proof that it is possible to be both big and beautiful.

Elephant Facts

African elephants are the world's biggest land mammals. The largest ever recorded reached a weight of 10,500kg (11.6 tons). This is not perhaps too surprising for an animal that can grow up to 4m (13ft 1in) tall. In fact, everything about these remarkable animals is huge. Their massive columnar feet can be up to 45cm (17.7in) across. These help to support the elephant's great weight, with a sole made from elastic layers of skin that absorbs pressure and allows this true giant to move remarkably quietly.

Their ears, too, are oversized, and designed to conduct away excess body heat quickly and efficiently, through a network of blood vessels close to the ear's surface. The final additions to this massive bulk are an elongated snout, called a trunk, and a set of massive incisor teeth (the tusks), which are grown by both male and females. The largest example of these 'overgrown teeth' can be found in the Natural History Museum, London and weigh 102kg (224.9lb) each. The combined weight of trunk and tusks is often so great that, even though the tusks are hollow, elephants can often be seen resting them on branches.

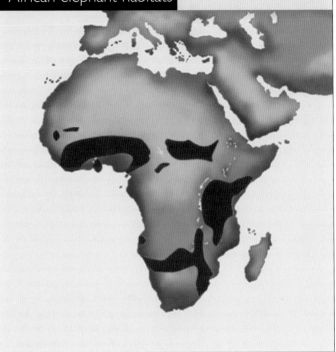

African elephant habitats

Mother Love

Elephant society is complex and highly structured. Generally, a herd comprises an enlarged family unit, made up of a group of up to 12 related females and their calves. The leader of the group is the oldest female, called the matriarch, who walks at the head of the herd as they travel – in a straight line – from range to range. Males tend to

Comparisons

Despite many similarities, it is relatively easy to tell the difference between an Asian elephant (*Elephas maximus*) and an African. Asian elephants are slightly smaller and paler, and only the male of the species grows tusks. Asian elephants are also much rarer than their African cousins. Due to habitat loss and poaching, Asian elephants are listed as 'Endangered' on the IUCN's Red List.

African elephant   Asiatic elephant

stay with the group until they reach around 12 years of age, when they are forced by the herd to leave. Juvenile bulls are often found living together in batchelor groups.

The heart of the herd is the young calves, who are dependent on their mother's care for the first two years of life. During that time, all of the herd's females will protect and feed the calves, acting as surrogate 'allomothers'. If danger threatens, the females circle around the calves and will actively challenge any would-be aggressor.

Threats and Conservation

The African elephant's closest ancestor is thought to be the woolly mammoth which became extinct 4000 years ago, and in the 1990s it seemed the elephant was about to disappear, too. In East Africa, for example, elephant numbers fell from 1.3 million in 1981 to 600,000 in 1990. African elephants were listed as 'Endangered' in the 1996 IUCN Red List, and, as a result of widespread public support, numerous laws were brought in to give them some degree of protection from extinction.

The most effective appears to have been the 1989 ban in the trade in ivory and elephant products. Although countries such as South Africa and Mozambique still allow a limited trade in hunting trophies, initial research seems to suggest that elephant numbers are slowly recovering. Illegal poaching is still a problem, as is loss of habitat, but the 2004 IUCN Red List now lists the status of elephants as 'Vulnerable'. This means that these large pachyderms still need our protection, but that the future is not looking quite as bleak for the African elephant.

African elephants are extremely caring mothers and a newborn receives lots of care and attention.

Baby elephants are able to walk an hour after they are born, but may need a helpful nudge to get started.

The mother elephant's trunk is used to give the calf both support and affection.

During the heat of the day, a large mother makes a useful sunshade!

African Wild Ass

Looking like a curious cross between a horse and a zebra, the African wild ass has the dubious distinction of being one of the world's rarest animals. It was once a common sight as far afield as Morocco, the Sudan, Somalia and the Arabian Peninsula, but now only small, isolated groups of this sure-footed mammal survive in the wild.

Teeth
The teeth of the wild ass show clearly that this species lives primarily on grass – with large, chisel-like incisors for cutting and flat, grinding teeth to help break up tough vegetation.

Key Facts	ORDER *Perissodactyla* / FAMILY *Equidae* GENUS & SPECIES *Equus asinus*
Weight	275kg (606lb)
Length	Head and body 2.1m (6ft 9in)
Tail	45cm (17.7in)
Shoulder height	1.4m (4ft 6in)
Sexual maturity	2 years, but rarely breeds before 4–5 years
Mating season	Peaks during wet season (July to August)
Gestation period	About 360 days
Number of young	1
Birth interval	1 year
Typical diet	Grazes grasses, sedges and forbs; browses shrubs and bushes
Life span	12–22 years

Domestic ass
Although they have shorter and stockier bodies, domestic asses are clearly descended from African wild asses. Like their free-roaming cousins, these hardy animals are natural beasts of burden.

Hooves
African wild asses have extremely narrow hooves, which enable them to walk steadily over uneven and rocky ground.

Ears
The African wild ass's large,
upright ears can be swivelled
around in almost any direction.
This helps it to keep track of
other members of the group.

The African ass (*Equus asinus*) is the wild version of the domestic donkey. Built to withstand the harsh conditions on Africa's sparsely vegetated scrublands, this naturally hardy little mammal has long been valued as a 'beast of burden' throughout the continent. Despite its value, there may be fewer than 570 left in the wild.

Horse of a Different Colour

Horses, asses and zebras all belong to the family Equidae and share a number of common traits: strong, muscular bodies, powerful hindquarters, hooves instead of feet, long necks, and eyes and ears placed high on a distinctive, almost triangular shaped head.

Despite these similarities, it is clear from their appearance that all three belong to different species. Asses are the smallest and stockiest of the three – growing to around 2m (6ft 6in) from head to tail and up to 275kg (606lb) in weight. Its mane is sparser and coarser than both that of the horse and zebra, its coat is generally grey to pale brown (which is darker in the dry season) and it has a white underbelly. Its two known subspecies, the Nubian wild ass (*Equus asinus africanus*) and the Somali wild ass (*Equus asinus somalicus*), also have some striping on the lower legs, like a zebra.

Desert Dwellers?

African wild asses are a hardy species and survive well in arid, semi-desert regions, hill and bush lands. Yet they are not natural desert dwellers. When food and water is scarce

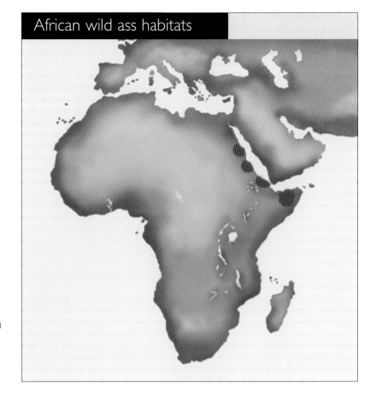

African wild ass habitats

it is possible for a wild ass to lose up to one-third of its body weight and still survive, but most family groups choose to live within 30km (18.6 miles) of a fresh water source. Expectant and feeding mothers in particular need to drink every day in order to remain healthy. To conserve moisture, asses often retreat to a cool, rocky outcrop during the hottest part of the day. In fact, they are generally

Comparisons

As these illustrations show, the Asiatic wild ass (*Equus hemionus*) is generally smaller than the African, with shorter legs, tail and ears. Like the African wild ass, Asiatic wild ass (*Equus hemionus*) populations have also fallen rapidly in recent decades. So much so that the five surviving subspecies of this small, brown-coated donkey are various classed as 'Vulnerable' and 'Endangered'.

Asiatic wild ass

African wild ass

In the cooler temperatures of early morning, a lone wild ass enjoys a leisurely breakfast.

The ass stops eating to investigate a figure on the horizon. Its raised ears indicate that it is alert to any potential trouble.

Each recognizing a family member, the asses touch snouts in a familiar greeting.

Head to tail, the asses may spend many minutes reinforcing old relationships with mutual grooming.

and nocturnal, which means that they are more active at dawn and at night, when temperatures are cooler.

Another clue to the fact that they are not natural desert inhabitants comes from their feet. Wild asses have a pointed, narrow hoof and tend to walk delicately on 'tiptoes'. This is ideal for the rocky and uneven terrain found at the edges of deserts, but bad on sand where broad, cushion-like pads, such those found on a camel's foot, are better at 'snow-ploughing' through the ever-shifting sand.

Threats and Conservation

During the 1980s, African wild ass numbers are believed to have fallen by as much as 50 per cent. Today, the species is classed as 'Critically Endangered', as are the Numbian and Somali wild asses. No one reason can be blamed for such a startling fall in the numbers of a once abundant

animal – rather, it is a combination of threats that has combined to bring this appealing little donkey to the brink of extinction.

In common with many equine species, wild asses have been captured and interbred with domestic species for centuries. Despite legal protection, they are routinely hunted for food and traditional medicines. Droughts and wars have taken their toll, too, while the growth of agriculture has restricted the animals' access to water, which is vital for its survival. The future of the wild ass hinges on a population of around 400, which is found in Eritrea. This is large enough to be considered 'viable', meaning that it is capable of sustaining and increasing its numbers. Asses are a resilient species, so it is possible that, given a stable and protective environment, the wild ass may yet live to roam Africa's bush lands once more.

African Wild Dog

With their large, rounded ears, tufted tails and mottled coats, African wild dogs are one of the most distinctive and appealing-looking members of the canine family. Once common throughout Africa's plains and savannahs, this sociable and attractive mini-predator is now facing extinction through much of its range.

Feet

These wild dogs are unique in that they have only four toes, instead of five. The dewclaw, which is sometimes referred to as the thumb, is missing in this species.

Coat

The Latin name for the African wild dog is *Lycaon pictus*. This means 'painted wolf' and refers to the yellow, black and white blotches on its coat, which are unique to each dog.

Key Facts	ORDER *Carnivora* / FAMILY *Canidae* GENUS & SPECIES *Lycaon pictus*
Weight	20–30kg (44–66lb)
Length Head and body Tail	75–100cm (30–40in) 30–40cm (12–16in)
Shoulder height	60–75cm (24–30in)
Sexual maturity	12–18 months
Mating season	Variable; when prey becomes locally abundant
Gestation period	70–75 days
Number of young	2–19; average 7–10
Birth interval	Roughly 1 year
Typical diet	Exclusively carnivorous; prefers big game, but will prey on hares, rodents and other small animals
Life span	About 10 years

A hundred years ago, the wiry, long-legged African wild dog would have been a common sight on the grassland plains and bushy savannahs of sub-Saharan Africa. Today, there may be as few as 4000 left in the world. Even in relatively protected environments, such as the Selous Game Reserve in Tanzania, there are believed to be fewer than 100 wild dogs.

A Family Affair

African wild dogs are sociable animals and live most of their lives in family groups. These groups are called 'packs', and are unusual in that all the males are related to each other and all the females are related to each other. This is because groups of related females leave the original group to form their own packs as soon as they reach maturity, which is at around two years of age. They will then join with another group of males to form a breeding pack. Although only the dominant males and females breed, this is an amazingly democratic society, and the pack works together to look after the young. As it may take up to six months before a juvenile is able to hunt for itself, this is very much a full-time job for the pack. In fact, the pups remain the group's top priority even once they are weaned and able to eat meat themselves, instead of relying on food that has been regurgitated by other members of the pack. They are even allowed to eat first – before the dominant male and female.

Threats

The main problem facing the African wild dog is the same as that facing much of Africa's wildlife in general: loss of habitat. As populations grow, farms and towns expand out

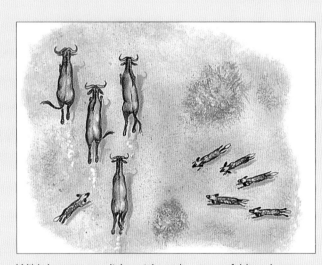

Wild dogs are too lightweight to be successful lone hunters, so they do what they do best – hunt in packs.

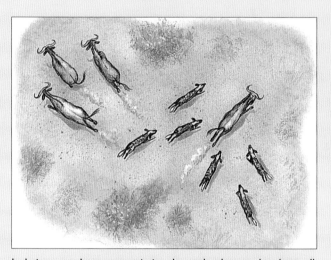

Isolating a weak or young victim, the pack takes up the chase, all the dogs using their incredible stamina to wear out the prey.

As the prey starts to tire and slow, the dogs bite at their victim's legs and belly.

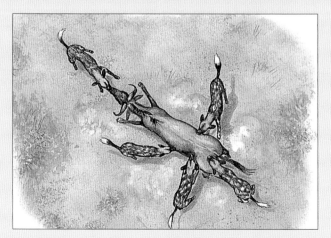

Eventually, injuries or exhaustion force the prey to collapse, allowing the wild dogs to move in for the kill.

into the countryside. Wild dogs are more adaptable than many other species, but they still suffer huge casualties as their traditional habitats are swallowed up by urbanization. As the available land shrinks, small, isolated wild dog packs are left without enough space in which to hunt.

The result is twofold. First, wild dogs are forced onto farmland, which puts them into direct conflict with humans. Secondly, they are forced to live in smaller and smaller and smaller packs. A healthy wild dog pack used to contain around 30 members. Now the average number is around 10. As packs rely on each other to find food, to baby-sit the young and to protect pups from predators, falling numbers make everyday living more difficult. African wild dogs are also susceptible to a variety of diseases, such as rabies and distemper, which they catch from domestic dogs.

Conservation

Despite legal protection, wild dogs are facing extinction in many countries. With so many more 'glamorous', high-profile animals under threat – and with resources stretched thin – wild dogs are generally not considered to be a priority. There are captive breeding programmes, but dogs reared in zoos often lack the necessary hunting skills to survive in the wild. Nature reserves have been of little help either. A dog pack can travel as much as 40 kilometres (25 miles) during the course of a hunt. Even in the largest nature reserves, this means that there simply is not enough space for the packs to roam freely.

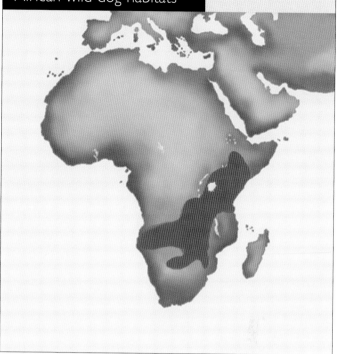

African wild dog habitats

The last lifeline for this beleaguered species, however, may well come from an unexpected source. In the past, people came to Africa to hunt the wildlife. Now they come to admire it. Ecotourism is a growing phenomenon around the world and in Africa in particular, and this curious, multicoloured little dog is proving to be a popular attraction with visitors.

Comparisons

It may be surprising, but African wild dogs belong to the family Canidae, which is the same family as domesticated dogs (*Canis familiaris*), such as the greyhound. In fact, dogs, coyotes, wolves, jackals and foxes all have a common ancestor called a *Tomarcyus*, which lived around 15 million years ago.

African wild dog

Greyhound

Aye-Aye

With its large ears, long, bushy tail and coarse black fur, the aye-aye looks like some strange cross between a squirrel and a bat. However, this large, curious-looking tree dweller is actually a primate. It was once thought to be extinct, and only a small number of these unique mammals now remain in the wild.

Key Facts	ORDER *Primates* / FAMILY *Daubentoniidae* GENUS SPECIES *Daubentonia madagascariensis*	
Weight	About 2kg (4lb 6oz)	
Length Head and body Tail	36–44cm (14–17in) 50–60cm (20–24in)	
Sexual maturity	2 years	
Mating season	Throughout the year	
Gestation period	160 days	
Number of young	Usually 1	
Birth interval	2–3 years	
Typical diet	Insect larvae and fruit	
Life span	Up to 26 years in captivity, unknown in the wild	

Hand
Aye-ayes have unusually long fingers and toes. The third digit on each hand is used to probe wood for insect larvae (grubs).

Ears
The aye-aye's large ears are specialist hunting tools. They work like radar dishes to help the aye-aye locate insect larvae moving around in tree trunks.

Hindfoot
In common with many arboreal species, especially primates, the aye-aye has an opposable big toe. This allows it to grip the tree branches securely.

Fur
An aye-aye's body is covered with a thick 'under fur' of rough hair – usually black or brown in colour – with an outer layer of coarse, white guard hairs on top.

Aye-ayes have the distinction of being the world's largest living nocturnal primate. Sadly, this most remarkable of nature's animals is also one of the rarest. Worldwide, one in five of all primates – a group that includes lemurs, monkeys and apes – is under threat of extinction, and it may be only a short time before this increasingly rare species vanishes entirely.

Tree Rats?

With their large, batlike ears, huge eyes and bony fingers, aye-ayes make a curious sight as they jump through the forest canopy foraging for food – something they do for up to 80 per cent of the night. Aye-ayes eat fruit, seeds and nectar, but their favourite food is wood-boring grubs, which they locate by tapping tree trunks with their elongated finger and listening for movement. Once a meal has been detected, aye-ayes use their front incisor teeth, like chisels, to strip away the wood. They then insert their elongated finger to fish out the larvae.

Such specialized behaviour is the result of thousands of years of 'adaptive evolution', which has made the aye-aye unique among primates. For example, aye-ayes have no canine teeth for tearing flesh, and no pre-molars for grinding vegetable matter, which is the norm in other primates. Instead, they have 22 close-set, continually growing molars. These are used to gnaw away at bark. This feature meant that aye-ayes used to be classified as rodents – the animal group that includes rats.

Legends and Omens

In his book *The Aye-Aye and I*, naturalist Gerald Durrell (1925–1995) described a particularly evocative encounter with an aye-aye:

'In the gloom it came along the branches towards me, its round, hypnotic eyes blazing, its spoon-like ears turning to and fro like radar dishes, its white whiskers twitching and moving like sensors; its black hands, with their thin fingers,

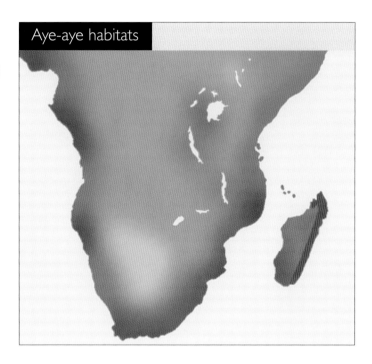

Aye-aye habitats

Comparisons

Scientists have been unable to agree as to whether aye-ayes are lemurs or belong to their own separate group. The Aye-aye may be slightly larger and darker in colour, as this illustration shows, but the two do look superficially similar. Also, both inhabit Madagascar's rainforests and woodlands and enjoy a comparable diet.

Greater dwarf lemur

Aye-aye

As the aye-aye's natural habitats are destroyed, many have moved into coconut plantations.

Coconuts are easy picking for the aye-ayes, whose powerful incisor teeth can easily break open the nut's tough outer shell.

Their long middle finger – so useful when hunting grubs – is equally handy when feasting on coconuts.

Using its elongated middle finger like a spoon, the aye-aye can scoop out the creamy coconut flesh with ease.

the third seeming terribly elongated, tapping delicately on the branches as it moved along.'

Is it any wonder, then, that this harmless mammal has become the subject of fear and superstition throughout its Madagascan homeland? Local people believe that the appearance of an aye-aye is an omen of bad luck. Some legends even claim that aye-ayes creep into homes during the night and use their skeletal middle finger to cut sleeper's throats! Such beliefs have not helped the aye-aye's fight for survival, although the actual number killed directly by humans is probably quite small by comparison to the deaths caused when their forest homelands are destroyed.

Threats and Conservation

The aye-aye is generally solitary, spending much of its time in the tree tops, where it sleeps throughout the day,

in large purpose-built nests. When foraging for food, it occasionally wanders into towns, but its natural habitats are woodlands, rainforests and mango swamps, which provide it with food, shelter and protection from predators. Unfortunately, these are precisely the areas that are being cleared throughout Madagascar, to make way for valuable sugar and coconut plantations.

For such a specialized animal, such rapid change has been devastating. It is believed there may be fewer than 1000 aye-ayes left on its island home. Aye-ayes are now protected by law, and a colony has been established on Nosy Mangabe, which is a reserve off Madagascar's north-eastern coast. However, aye-ayes breed slowly – giving birth just once every two or three years. Eight Madagascan animals became extinct in 2004, so it may only be a matter of time before this creature is added to the list.

Black Rhino

Black rhinoceroses are one of Africa's most famous and impressive wild inhabitants. Large, fearsome and with few natural enemies, they should be facing a secure future, but changes in land use, war, civil unrest and poverty continue to threaten their security.

Feet

The rhinoceros is an odd-toed ungulate (or hoofed animal). Its feet are tridactyl, which means that it has three hooves on each foot. These huge hooves (of which the middle is the largest) sit on columnar legs and help to spread the rhino's weight.

Key Facts	ORDER *Perissodactyla*
	FAMILY *Rhinocerotidae*
	GENUS & SPECIES *Diceros bicornis*

Weight	1360–1815kg (2998–3999lb)
Length Head and body Tail	 3–3.8m (9ft 10in–12ft 6in) 68cm (26.7in)
Front horn	45–127cm (17.7–50in)
Shoulder height	1.4–1.6m (4ft 6in–5ft 3in)
Sexual maturity	Female 4–6 years; male 7–9 years
Mating season	Throughout the year
Gestation period	419–478 days
Number of young	1
Birth interval	2–5 years
Typical diet	Leaves, buds and shoots of small trees and bushes; herbs, clover and fruit
Life span	30–40 years

Lips

Black rhinos are sometimes called 'hook-lipped' rhinos due to their pointed, prehensile upper lip. This is used to grasp vegetation as the rhino eats. White rhinos are known as 'square-lipped'.

Black rhinoceroses belong to the family Rhinocerotidae. They share many features with the hippopotamus, Africa's other large, hoofed ungulate; however, hippos are related to pigs, while rhinos have more in common with horses.

Messy Memos

Black rhinoceroses are herbivores, living on a wide variety of thorny bushes, leaves and shoots, which they carefully pluck with their prehensile lips. These bulky creatures are generally solitary, making their homes in a wide variety of habitats, where a suitable food supply is available. The females of the species are not particularly territorial, but males may occupy overlapping ranges, which they mark with heaps of dung and urine. Many male animals mark their territory in some way. Birds use song to declare their ownership of a specific territory. Other animals have musk glands, which they rub against trees and rocks to let competitors know that they have passed through. Others scent-mark the area, spraying urine along the edges of

their territory. This may sound odd, but marking the borders of their range makes good sense: it keeps out intruders and reduces unwanted conflict.

Weapons and Armour

The word 'rhinoceros' comes from two Greek words meaning 'nose' and 'horn', and it is these double horns that are the black rhinoceros's most distinctive features. These

Comparisons

Up to 50 per cent larger than the black rhinoceros, white rhinos (*Ceratotherium simum*) are the largest land-dwelling species, after elephants and about the same size as hippos.

Despite their name, white rhinos are not white at all, but blue-grey in colour, just like black rhinos. Their name comes from the Afrikaans word for 'wide', which refers to their mouth.

Black rhino

White rhino

Although solitary for most of the year, male and female rhinos come together every two or three years to mate.

Mating may take place at any time during the year, but activity peaks in the rainy season, when food is plentiful.

huge spikes are used mainly for defence and display, although the larger, longer front horn may also be used to dig up shrubs and grasses. True horns, such as those grown by deer, are solid and embedded in the skull. The base of these, however, are hollow masses of matted keratin (a hairlike substance), which are embedded in the skin.

Asian Sumatran rhinoceroses (*Dicerorhinus sumatrensis*) have a mass of wiry reddish hair, but African species, such as the black, are hairless. Instead, their skin is armour-thick and gives the impression of hanging in folds, where it creases at the joints. Surprisingly, this skin is not black but grey, although the actual colour varies depending on the type of mud in which the rhino wallows. These wallows keep the rhino cool and free of parasites, as do egrets, which can often be seen pecking the rhino's thick hide to remove ticks.

Threats and Conservation

There are four known subspecies of black rhinoceros: the south-western (*Diceros bicornis*), the western (*Diceros bicornis longipes*), the eastern (*Diceros bicornis michaeli*) and the south central black (*Diceros bicornis minor*). These great mammals once roamed through much of sub-Saharan Africa. However, centuries of overhunting have been their downfall and, by the 1990s, there were just a few thousand black rhinos remaining.

Although the black rhino's horns are used in Chinese medicine, it is the ivory trade that has had the biggest impact on its numbers – especially the popularity of ceremonial daggers called jambiyas. Trade in rhino horn

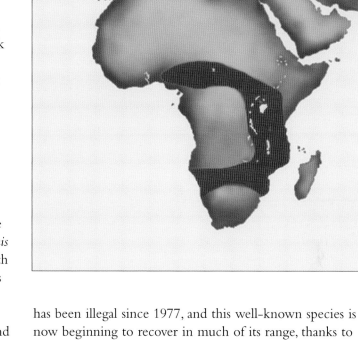

Black rhino habitats

has been illegal since 1977, and this well-known species is now beginning to recover in much of its range, thanks to careful management and the strict enforcement of legal protections. Yet poverty continues to tempt poachers, and remaining black rhinoceros populations are secure only in a fraction of their former territory, in protected reserves in Kenya, South Africa, Namibia and Zimbabwe.

Females reach sexual maturity at around four to six years of age and give birth to one calf at a time.

After mating, gestation takes around sixteen months. The young calf will stay with its mother until a new baby arrives.

Chimpanzee

It is the chimpanzee's playfulness and natural curiosity that makes it seem so amazingly 'human'. And this is more than just a passing resemblance. These great apes actually share 98.4 per cent of our DNA – the molecule that carries our genetic makeup. This makes these intelligent and sociable animals our closest living ancestor. A good enough reason, if there were no other, to protect a species that is increasingly threatened with extinction.

Key Facts	ORDER *Primates* / FAMILY *Pongidae* GENUS & SPECIES *Pan troglodytes*	
Weight	27–68kg (60–150lb)	
Height	1–1.5m (3ft 3in–4ft 9in)	
Sexual maturity	7 years, but does not breed until 12–15 years old	
Mating season	All year	
Gestation period	230 days	
Number of young	1	
Birth interval	3 years, often longer	
Typical diet	Fruit, leaves, berries, nuts, insects and, occasionally, mammals and birds	
Life span	Up to 60 years	

Teeth

The combination of flat, grinding molars and sharp, cutting incisors tell us that chimpanzees, like humans, are omnivores. They eat both meat and vegetables.

Feet

The chimpanzee's feet have long, muscular toes, with one big toe that acts like a thumb, enabling the chimpanzee to grasp objects securely.

Hands and arms

Chimpanzees' arms are longer than their legs. This produces a rolling motion when they walk on all fours. They also climb well using their powerful hands and arms to swing through the canopy.

There are four known subspecies of chimpanzee: the western masked (*Pan troglodytes verus*), the eastern long-haired (*Pan troglodytes schweinfurthii*), the eastern Nigerian (*Pan troglodytes vellerosus*) and the central black-faced chimpanzee (*Pan troglodytes troglodytes*). Although chimp populations vary throughout Africa, all four subspecies are considered to be endangered, with fewer than 1000 individuals remaining, even in relatively secure regions such as the Mahale Mountain National Park in Tanzania.

A Life Aloft

When chimpanzees walk on all fours, they do not put their full weight on their hands like true quadrupeds. Instead, they support their upper body on their knuckles, and use the sides of the feet to take the rest of the weight. As their arms are longer than their legs, they move with a long, rolling gait, and are capable of moving surprisingly quickly. They can – and do – occasionally walk on two legs, although it is usually only males who do this, to exert dominance over the troop.

For most of the time, though, chimps are content to lie among the tree tops. It is here that they sleep during the night, making huge nests out of branches and leaves. During the day, when they have finished feeding, they also use the trees as a place to relax and digest. They come down to the ground for short times only, either foraging for food or grooming other members of the troop, which is an important part of chimp social life. In fact, they spend only around a half of their day on the ground, which may seem surprising, but just one look at a chimpanzee will tell you that this is an animal designed primarily for a life among the tree tops.

During the day, chimpanzee troops split into small groups, called 'parties', to search for food.

Using their dexterous feet to grip branches, party members shake nuts and fruit loose.

Other members of the party gather up the fallen nuts. Fruit, roots, seeds, termites and, often, small mammals form a valuable part of the diet, too.

Chimpanzees are skilled tool users and use large stones to break open the tough shells of nuts.

No Place Like Home

In common with many tree dwellers, chimps have powerful arms and legs, with especially flexible shoulder joints that allow them to swing through the canopy with apparent ease. Their hands are extremely long and dexterous – ideal for grabbing and holding onto branches. Their bodies are light and muscular and, while they do not have tails, their dexterous feet are just as useful in helping them to keep their balance in the treetops.

It is this reliance on the forest that has caused species numbers to fall so dramatically over the past few decades. Chimpanzees make their homes in the dense rainforests and dry savannah woodlands that form a lush, green, broad belt across Western and Central Africa. As the forests disappear, however, chimpanzees have nowhere else to go.

Threats and Conservation

Logging, farming and the growth of towns and cities has resulted in wide-scale deforestation throughout Africa. Such developments have left small pockets of forest, isolated from each other. This means that chimps must risk encountering humans when travelling through their traditional territories, and this is an increasingly dangerous thing for them to do. Chimpanzee body parts are used in traditional medicines, but chimps also represent a cheap and easy source of food. In fact, the trade in so-called 'bush meat' is growing rapidly, and not only is this being eaten by the local population, but it is increasingly exported abroad as well. Some environmentalists believe

that this trade is the greatest current threat to chimpanzee survival. Whatever the dangers, the future for our forest brothers looks bleak. These sociable and expressive primates are protected by law throughout Africa. Yet the areas that they inhabit are so remote and so large that enforcing these laws is difficult and chimpanzee numbers continue to fall.

Chimpanzee habitats

Comparisons

Like chimpanzees, mountain gorillas and western and eastern lowland gorillas are falling rapidly in number as their natural forest habitats are stripped away to make space for expanding towns and cities. In fact, all four of the 'great apes' – chimpanzees, bonobos, orang-utans and gorillas – are classed as 'Endangered' on the 2004 IUCN's Red List.

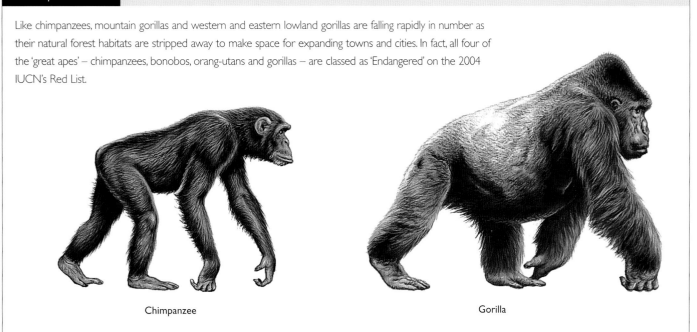

Chimpanzee   Gorilla

Ethiopian Wolf

This attractive canine is Africa's only native species of wolf, and one which is becoming increasingly rare. With fewer than 500 individuals left in the wild, time is running out for this red-coated hunter.

Muzzle
The Ethiopian wolf's muzzle is somewhat longer and thinner than those of other species of wolf. This enables it to forage deep in burrows, in search of small prey.

Key Facts

	ORDER *Carnivora* / FAMILY *Canidae* / GENUS & SPECIES *Canis simensis*
Weight	11.2–19kg (24–42lb)
Length Head and body	100cm (39in)
Shoulder height	58cm (23in)
Tail length	33cm (13in)
Sexual maturity	2 years
Breeding season	October–January
Gestation period	60–62 days
Number of young	2–6
Birth interval	1 year
Typical diet	Small mammals
Lifespan	8–9 years

Legs
With its long, slender legs, this canine looks remarkably similar to the maned wolf (*Chrysocyon brachyurus*), which lives in Latin America.

Tail

The Ethiopian wolf's dark tipped, bushy tail is a characteristic of not only many other species of wolf, but also of some of the larger domestic dogs such as German shepherds.

Wolf numbers have been declining worldwide ever since they began to come into conflict with humans. At first wolves, particularly the large, grey wolf of North America and Europe were simply considered to be a pest who would take farm animals if the opportunity presented itself. Later their reputation grew more sinister or fearful, and they began to be associated with everything dark and dangerous. No wonder, then, that so few wolf populations remain.

All Together Now

Ethiopian wolves are generally sociable animals, they live in small packs of between three and thirteen individuals. This family groups includes males, females and young pups. Typically, the males are born into the pack and stay with it through out their lives. To avoid interbreeding, however, females will leave the pack either permanently or temporarily – to mate with males from other, packs.

When the pups are born, these tiny 200g (7oz) balls of fur are incredibly vulnerable. It will be almost six months before they can start to hunt for themselves, so their mother and other members of the pack take turns in feeding the hungry pups. The pack also help to defend the group from predators and other wolf packs by regularly patrolling and scent-marking territorial boundaries.

Top Dogs

Ethiopian wolves reach sexual maturity at around two years of age and will generally mate just once a year. In a

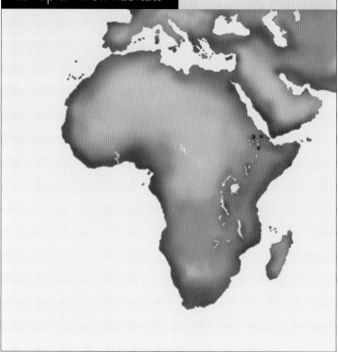

Ethiopian wolf habitats

wolf pack, however, 'status' is all-important. Only the dominant females generally mate, although other females will take a turn in caring and feeding for the young. Usually, only the 'top dog' will do as a suitor, although, if a female mates outside the pack, she is less choosy.

After mating, it takes around nine weeks before the new season's pups are born – usually two to six per litter. To keep

Comparisons

Wolves are believed to be one of the ancestors of domestic dogs. In fact, when you compare the Ethiopian wolf with the coyote (*Canis latrans*), which is a wild dog, rather than a wolf, the resemblance is clear. Despite the fact that coyotes live on North American rather than African grasslands, both have a very similar body design, with their long legs, narrow muzzle and large ears.

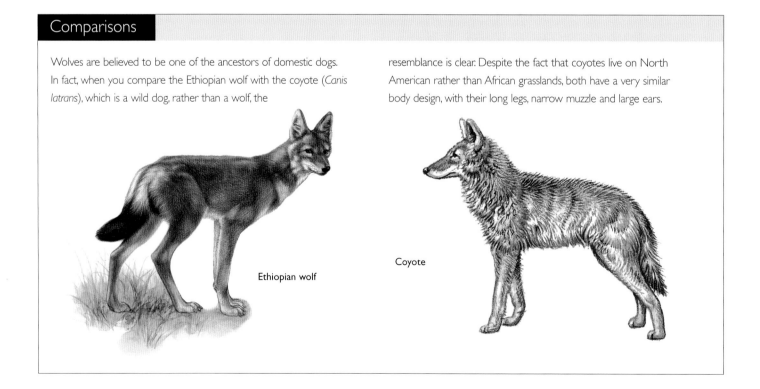

Ethiopian wolf

Coyote

them safe, the female guards them in an underground den which may have several different entrances. She may even move dens every few weeks if she feels particularly unsafe. It is here that the pups will spend their first month, when they are entirely dependent on their mother's milk for food. After that, they will begin to eat solid foods and start to learn the rules and regulations of life in the pack.

Threats and Conservation

One of the biggest threats to the Ethiopian wolf's continued survival is – as is the case through much of Africa – the loss of land to farming. Around 60 per cent of the wolves' traditional habitat has now been lost and what remains is vulnerable to overgrazing. The increase in farming has also exacerbated a problem which has been growing since the 1980s. Many farmers in the region routinely use dogs to protect their sheep; however, these animals are generally allowed to run wild. This means that they not only compete with the wolves for food, but they also interbreed with them, and pass on diseases such as rabies and distemper to the wolf population.

Recently a number of organizations, including the Born Free Foundation, have begun to address some of these problems. Domestic dogs have been vaccinated and hybrids have been sterilized to prevent them from further contaminating the gene pool. The rest of the programme depends on educating local people about value of their wolves and protecting remaining habitats. Populations are still declining, however, and time may be running out for Africa's only native wolf.

Although Ethiopian wolves live in packs, they go out to hunt for food on their own.

This is possible because up to 90 per cent of their diet is made up of small mammals, such as rats and the occasional hare.

After tracking a potential meal, the wolf uses its front paws to dig down, where the rat has taken refuge in its underground burrow.

The Ethiopian wolf's long, narrow muzzle and widely spaced teeth are the ideal tools for helping it to capture small mammals.

Mountain Gorilla

The mountain gorilla was first discovered in 1847. Since then these great apes have become famous, thanks mainly to the work of zoologist Dian Fossey (1932–1985) and the film *Gorillas in the Mist*. Although Dian was murdered, probably by poachers who objected to her stance on animal conservation, her foundation continues her work. With their help and these of other ape friends, it may not be too late to save the mountain gorilla.

Arms
It is difficult for a gorilla to stand upright. Instead, it generally walks on all fours, using the knuckles of its hands to support its weight.

Head
Only male gorillas have the distinctive high-browed 'sagittal' (arrow-like) crest on their head. This ridge is attached to the gorilla's massive jaw muscles.

Key Facts

ORDER *Primates* / FAMILY *Hominadae* / GENUS & SPECIES *Gorilla gorilla berengei*

Weight	120–227kg (265–500lb)
Length Head and body	Upright, males reach 1.5–1.7m (5–6ft)
Sexual maturity	Female 7–8 years, male 12–15 years
Breeding season	Throughout the year, 3 days each month
Number of young	1
Gestation period	8 months
Birth interval	6–8 years
Typical diet	Vegetarian, includes bamboo, wild celery, thistles, stinging nettles and fruit
Life span	50 years in the wild, 53 years in captivity

Fur
Gorillas usually have thick, glossy fur all over their bodies, apart from on their face, the palms of the hands, the soles of the feet and on their chests.

Gorillas are the biggest and strongest members of the anthropoid (meaning 'human-like') ape family. This is a group which includes orang-utans and chimpanzees. Sadly, with fewer than 400 individuals left in the wild, the mountain gorilla has now joined its fellow apes on the growing list of endangered species.

Gentle Giants

Despite their size, gorillas are far from being 'big, dumb apes'. In fact, they have a much-deserved reputation for being gentle and thoughtful creatures.

As an example, when, in 1986, a young boy fell into the gorilla enclosure at Jersey Zoo, on the Channel island of Jersey, the action of the gorilla Jambo made news headlines. As the anguished crowd watched, Jambo went to investigate the unconscious figure. After stroking the boy's

face Jambo then stood watch over his unconscious form until leaving voluntarily when the keepers entered the enclosure. Naturalist Gerald Durrell, who founded the zoo, later hailed Jambo as a 'magnificent individual' whose presence kept some of the more boisterous members of the troop in check. And this was not an isolated incident. Ten years later in Chicago, TV viewers in the United States watched astounded as a female gorilla cradled in her arms a boy who had fallen into the enclosure. Gorillas have also been taught to 'speak' using sign language, displaying a remarkable level of intelligence and perseverance in the process.

Black and Silver

Typically mountain gorillas live in small family groups of one or two adult males (over 12 years of age), females and infants. The head of the troupe is the 'silverback' – a dominant male who can usually be identified by the patch of grey hair on his back. Younger males who lack this distinguishing feature are known as 'blackbacks'.

The silverback is generally the oldest and largest male in the group. He is the one who leads the daily treks in

Comparisons

As these illustrations show, female mountain gorillas are much smaller than males. In fact, an adult silverback can be twice the weight of his mate. Mountain gorillas are the largest of all primates and, standing upright, are easily able to look an average-sized man straight in the eyes.

An average day for a mountain gorilla begins just after dawn, when the troop, led by the silverback, sets off in search of a meal.

search of food, and who protects the group from danger. He is also the centre of attention during rest periods when the troop take time out to groom one another. As dominant male, the silverback is usually the only male who has the right to breed with the females, and most of the babies in the troop will belong to this big daddy.

Threats and Conservation

It is a sad fact that almost all of our closest relatives – the apes – are now listed as 'Endangered'. In the case of the mountain gorilla, the situation has now reached critical levels. Their survival depends entirely on the continued existence of the mountain forests in which these magnificent animals make their homes. In the past gorillas were hunted for their meat and body parts, which have been used in traditional medicines. Today, the greatest threat to this great primate is war. Since 1990 the region has been wracked by civil unrest, and refugee camps have sprung up in many parts of the gorillas' traditional homelands. Hunting and deforestation have followed. There are signs that populations are increasing, but its still too early to tell if these increases will be enough to save this gentle giant.

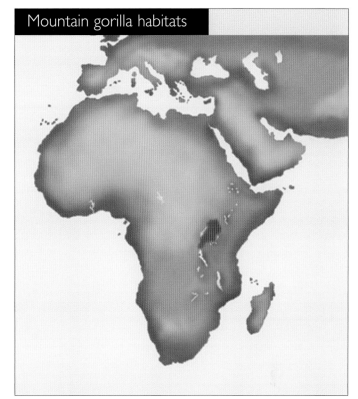

Mountain gorilla habitats

A gorilla's favourite foods are leaves, flowers, berries and fruit. Gorillas in zoos have been seen to eat meat but not very often.

After a foraging session, the troop usually takes a mid-morning rest. Often, as the adults snooze in makeshift nests, the juveniles play.

ARCTIC
OCEAN

KARA SEA

Central Siberian
Plateau

ASIA

Ural Mts

Lake
Baikal

SEA
OF
OKHOTS

Mongolia

Tien Shan Mts

Gobi
Desert

Plateau
of Tibet

Himalayas

Asia

Asia is home to three-fifths of the world's population
and covers 30 per cent of our planet's total landmass. It stretches from the
snow-tipped mountains of Tibet to the sun-kissed shores of the Indian
Ocean, and no continent is larger or more diverse.

~

Here you will find some of the world's highest mountains, driest deserts and lushest rainforests – each providing a unique habitat for the region's wildlife. Elephants, rhinos, camels, tigers and pandas all call this vast continent home. But it is a home that is becoming increasingly dangerous.

In 2004, the IUCN Red List included 330 Chinese, 306 Indian and 450 Indonesian species among those currently considered 'Endangered', 'Critically Endangered' or 'Vulnerable'. The reasons behind these statistics are not always easy to explain, but by far the greatest threat facing this burgeoning continent is deforestation. Between 1960 and 1990, Asia lost one-third of its tropical forests and, as these vanished, so, too, did the animals who relied on these green highways for food, shelter and protection. Much of this problem has been caused by illegal logging, yet with a billion people living in India alone, farming, industrialization and pollution are also taking their toll.

However, the news is not all bad. The growth in ecotourism has given people in the region tangible economic reasons to become 'animal friendly'. Increasingly, too, people are beginning to appreciate their continent's incredible 'natural' resources and to realize what a poorer world it would be without them.

Asian Elephant

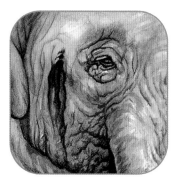

Since the American showman P.T. Barnum (1810–1891) made Jumbo the Elephant his star attraction, people have been fascinated by these intelligent and gregarious animals. It is hard to imagine a world without them, but as numbers continue to fall, this is exactly what may soon happen.

Musth gland

For around three months of the year, adult male elephants secrete a black fluid from a gland between the ear and eye. This indicates they are in 'musth' and are ready to mate.

Skull

The Asian elephant's skull is huge, comprising around 15 per cent of the elephant's entire body weight. It has to be this big to support the weight of the enormous trunk and tusks.

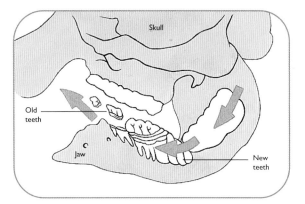

Feet

The elephant's massive columnar feet help to support its great weight, with a sole made from elastic layers of skin that absorb pressure and allow this true giant to move quietly and gracefully.

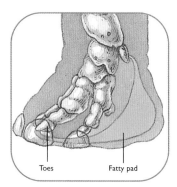

Key Facts	ORDER *Proboscidea* / FAMILY *Elephantidae* / GENUS & SPECIES *Elephas maximus*
Weight	Male up to 5.4 tons (6 tonnes); female up to 3.2 tons (3.5 tonnes)
Length	5.5–6.4m (18–21ft)
Shoulder height	Male 2.5–3m (8ft 2in–10ft); female 2.4–2.6m (7ft 10in–8ft 6in)
Sexual maturity	About 10 years
Mating season	End of rainy season to start of dry season
Gestation period	19–22 months
Number of young	Usually 1
Birth interval	About 4 years
Typical diet	Grasses, leaves, bamboo, plantains, bark
Life span	Up to 60 years on average, rarely 70–80

Asian elephant habitats

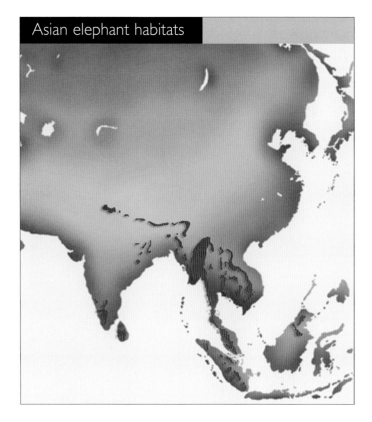

The Asian elephant is the Indian subcontinent's largest animal, and second only in size to its gigantic African cousin. These great beasts have suffered for centuries at the hands of humans and, although they are now protected, their future is still uncertain.

Eat Your Greens

Elephants are the world's largest living land animal. Head to tail, a male Asian elephant measures up to 6.4m (21ft) and stands almost 3m (almost 10ft) from toe to shoulder. Only giraffes are taller. Yet, they are not the largest creature on our planet. That distinction goes to the blue whale, which is 30m (98ft 5in) long. That is almost five times the length of an Asian elephant, making it the largest animal which has ever lived.

What might be surprising is that all these giants grow to such great heights without eating meat. Blue whales live almost entirely on a type of plankton called krill, giraffes eat leaves, while elephants fuel their massive bulk by munching their way through around 150kg (330lb) of grass, twigs and bark every day. When foraging, elephants can be quite destructive, and will push down trees and dig up shrubs to get a tasty meal. They are also partial to fruit such as coconuts, dates and sugar cane, which often leads them to raid farmers' fields when other food sources are scarce.

Gods and Monsters

Elephant power existed in India long before the arrival of bulldozers and Caterpillar tracks. These gentle animals are very intelligent and have been trained and used in the subcontinent for five thousand years to lift, carry and perform hundreds of other useful tasks. Even in the twenty-first century, around 15,000 domesticated elephants are still used to do jobs in areas where wheels and engines

Comparisons

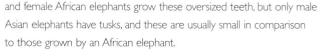

African elephants (*Loxodonta africana*) are the largest members of the elephant family. They are instantly recognizable by their ears, which are shaped a little like the African continent. They also lack the slightly humped back and prominent forehead of their Asian cousins, but the biggest difference between the two species is their tusks. Both male and female African elephants grow these oversized teeth, but only male Asian elephants have tusks, and these are usually small in comparison to those grown by an African elephant.

Asian
elephant

African
elephant

are unable to operate. However, elephants have played more than just an important economic role in India. They are part of the fabric of the nation, and feature in both folklore and religion. In Hinduism, for example, believers worship a supreme spirit who has no form or gender. To aid worship, images are used to represent aspects of the deity, including Ganesha, an elephant-headed god. Fitting with the character of the elephant who works for others' benefit, Ganesha is believed to be able to remove obstacles from the path of the believer.

Threats and Conservation

Historically, Asian elephants made their homes across a wide region, from the banks of the river Tigris, which borders Syria and Iraq, to the Yangtze River in Northern China. Today, the majority of these majestic mammals are found primarily in the Indian subcontinent, with smaller isolated populations in Indonesia, Laos, Malaysia, Thailand and Vietnam. Separate subspecies can be found in Sri Lanka (*Elephas maximus maximus*), Sumatra (*Elephas maximus sumatrensis*) and Borneo (*Elephas maximus borneensis*). In total, there are believed to be around 38,000 to 51,000 Asian elephants in the wild.

Hunting, which was so devastating to Asian elephant populations during the early twentieth century, is now less of a problem, but numbers are continuing to fall as traditional elephant habits are turned over to agriculture. As Asia's population continues to grow, the only hope for the elephant's continued survival is in finding ways for humans and their elephant helpers to coexist.

The elephant's flexible trunk makes a good tool for pulling up grass and shrubs.

The trunk also gives the elephant extra height to help it reach the leaves at the top of the tree.

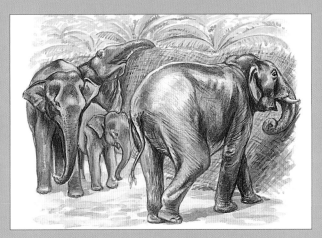

When food is scarce, farmers' fields and plantations are a tempting find.

A hungry herd of elephants can destroy all of a farmer's hard work in a single night.

Bactrian Camel

Although millions of domesticated Bactrian camels can be found throughout the Asian continent, the original feral Bactrian is now 'Critically Endangered'. Just a few wild herds remain in the desolate, parched sand and scrublands of the Gobi and Gashun deserts.

Nose
Bactrian camels have slit-like nostrils that can be closed tightly to stop them from inhaling lots of sand during a sandstorm.

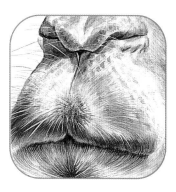

Key Facts	ORDER *Artiodactyla* / FAMILY *Camelidae* GENUS & SPECIES *Camelus bactrianus*
Weight	300–690kg (661–1521lb)
Length Head and body Tail	2.3–3.5m (7ft 6in–11ft 6in) 55cm (22in)
Shoulder height	1.8–2.3m (5ft 11in–7ft 6in)
Sexual maturity	5 years
Mating season	February–March
Gestation period	370–440 days
Number of young	Usually 1
Birth interval	2–3 years
Typical diet	Grasses and shrubs
Life span	Up to 50 years

Eyes

Exceptionally long eyelashes
and raised eyebrows help
to keep gritty sand out of
the camel's large eyes during
sandstorms in the desert.

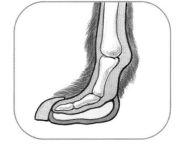

Feet

Camels have two toes on each foot,
connected by cushion-like pads which
spread out on the sand to support their
weight. Moving the two left legs, then the
two right legs together, camels walk with
a rolling motion, which has led to the
nickname 'ship of the desert'.

Comparisons

Like the Bactrian camel, the Asiatic wild ass (*Equus hemionus*) can be found in the arid regions of Central Asia. Both are good desert survivalists, able to tolerate extreme temperatures and to go for long periods without food and drink. However, the ass has solid hooves, which are better on rocky scrubland than the shifting sands of the desert.

Asiatic wild ass

Bactrian camel

Bactrian camels belong to the family Camelidae, and belong to the same animal order as llamas – the Latin American beast of burden. Despite their hard-working reputation, there may be fewer than 1000 Bactrian camels left in the wild.

Fuel Tanks

The camel is perfectly adapted for a life in the desert. Its feet, for example, have two toes on each foot, joined by a broad cushion-like pad. This spreads out as the camel walks, a little like a snowshoe, to support its weight. Its nostrils are thin, slitlike openings, which can be closed tight against sandstorms. Their eyes are also protected by giant eyelashes and a heavy brow. It is the camel's humps, though, which are its most remarkable desert survival tool.

Camels can travel for weeks with little or no water, but when they do drink they can take in 200L (211 quarts) a day. It used to be believed that they stored water in their humps because of this. They do not, but the humps are a valuable fuel reserve, storing fat, which provides energy when food is scarce. A healthy Bactrian camel's humps are pyramid-shaped and firm, but, if the animal is starving, the hump looks 'deflated' and may even hang to one side.

Domestic Bliss

Bactrian camels were first domesticated around 4500 years ago in Bactria, which is part of modern-day Afghanistan. For centuries, these hardy ungulates were used to carry luxury goods from China to the Middle East along the great Silk Road. Today, they are still an important source of transportation in regions where trucks and cars would soon get bogged down in sand.

And even when dead, these sure-footed beast of burden are a valued resource. In fact, a camel is a walking storehouse. Their wool and leather can be used to make warm and durable materials, such as clothing, blankets and tents. Their bones can be carved into jewellery and decorative items. Their meat is popular in a range of traditional dishes. Even their droppings have a use as fuel. All that explains why there are around 2.5 million domesticated Bactrian camels in Central Asia.

Threats and Conservation

Domestic Bactrian camels are quite different from their wild cousins. Centuries of selective breeding have made them bigger and stronger, with larger, irregular-shaped humps and darker coats. The success of these relative newcomers has placed such pressure on the few remaining wild Bactrian camel herds that they are simply unable to compete for food and resources with such large numbers of their domesticated relatives. To add to their problems, remaining wild herds are also hunted as an easy source of food by settlers who have moved into the desert to mine, extract oil and lay gas pipelines.

Reserves have now been established in both Mongolia (the Great Gobi A Reserve) and China (Arjin Shan Lop Nur reserve), in order to protect remaining wild camel populations. The most urgent need is for a breeding programme, as there are currently only 15 Bactrian camels in captivity. This means that, should a disaster wipe out the few remaining wild herds, the species would be lost to the world for ever.

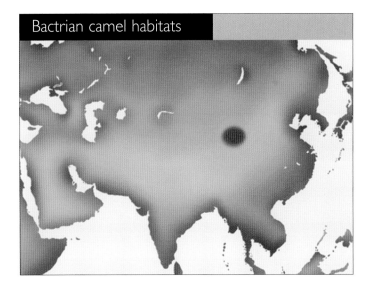

Bactrian camel habitats

Bactrian camels live either alone or in herds of up to 15 members. These herds have become much smaller in recent years due to hunting.

Individuals in the herd keep cool by pressing against the bodies of their comrades, as they are cooler than the surrounding air.

The herd may walk many kilometres in search of food, and must be able to cope with the extremes of desert weather.

The camel's long desert trek is broken up by regular stops to rest and sleep.

Giant Panda

Giant pandas are considered to be one of China's, if not the world's, greatest treasures. This high-profile bear has become a beacon for worldwide conservation efforts and a symbol of the World Wide Fund for Nature. With their teddy bear looks and gentle nature, giant pandas are perhaps the most famous of the world's endangered species.

Coat

Until 1901, giant pandas were known as 'mottled bears' due to their distinctive coat patterns. This bold banding acts as a natural camouflage to break up the outline of the panda's body shape.

Key Facts

ORDER *Carnivora* / FAMILY *Ursidae*
GENUS & SPECIES *Ailuropoda melonoleuca*

Weight	100–125kg (220–275lb)
Length	
Head and body	1.22–1.52m (4–5ft)
Tail	12–15cm (4.7–6in)
Shoulder height	51–64cm (20–25in)
Sexual maturity	5–7 years
Mating season	April–May
Gestation period	90–165 days
Number of young	Up to four but usually one or two
Birth interval	2 years
Typical diet	Almost exclusively bamboo stems; very rarely small animals, including fish
Life span	25–30 years

Eyes

In Chinese, the giant panda is called *Xiongmao*, which means 'giant cat bear'. This is a reference to its eyes, which have vertical slits, like those of a cat.

Teeth

Although giant pandas are natural carnivores, their teeth consist mainly of flat molars, which are more useful for grinding up vegetation than tearing at flesh.

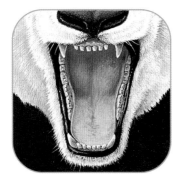

Paw

In common with red pandas, giant pandas have partially retractable claws. There is also an elongated wrist bone on each forepaw, which can be used like a thumb to help the panda hold objects securely.

There are two known subspecies of giant panda: the well-known black-and-white variety and the lesser known, and rarer, dark and light brown version, *Ailuropoda melanoleuca qinlingensis*. About 1600 giant pandas are currently believed to survive in the wild.

Parenting Problems

Giant pandas reproduce very slowly. It takes up to seven years before they reach sexual maturity, and most females give birth only every three or four years. Up to four cubs may be born at one time, but in captivity it is rare for the mother to attempt to raise more than one. Little is understood about their behaviour in the wild, but it is unknown for giant panda mothers to rear more than two cubs successfully. These newborns are extremely dependent on their mother. Almost naked, blind and weighing no more than 200g (7oz), they are not weaned before 11 weeks, and it is 18 weeks before they become completely independent. During this time, the babies are at constant risk from predators, especially as pandas do not build hidden dens, but shelter in rock or tree hollows. Such a low birth rate and survival rate have left giant panda populations even more vulnerable to the additional problems caused by hunting and habitat loss.

The Bamboo Bear

There are few mammals who have such a specialized diet as the giant panda. Naturally, this heavy-bodied bear is a

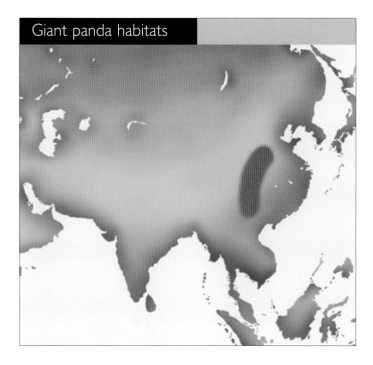

Giant panda habitats

carnivore, but in the wild it survives almost entirely on a diet of bamboo – a form of fibrous grass that grows up to 37m (121ft 5in) in height. Bamboo is a poor food source, and the panda's carnivore digestive system is able to extract only a small percentage of the plant's nutrients. This means that giant pandas must eat huge amounts – up to 38kg (94lb) – of bamboo every day in order to get enough energy to thrive.

Comparisons

Like their distant relatives, the red pandas, giant pandas were once classified as members of the racoon family Procyonidae. Genetic testing has now revealed what seems to be obvious when you look at the panda – that it is a bear. Like its relative the North American grizzly bear (*Ursus arctos*), the panda has the same squat limbs, broad body and long snout. The grizzly, though, is the true 'giant' of the family, growing to four–five times the weight of an average panda.

Giant panda

Grizzly bear

Bamboo is unusual in that it periodically flowers, produces seeds, then dies out. In ordinary situations, this would not be a problem – the panda would simply move to another feeding ground. As agriculture and illegal logging expand, however, giant panda populations have been squeezed into small mountain enclaves. Between 1974 and 1976, 138 pandas starved because the bamboo died out and the bears had no alternative food source in their range.

Threats and Conservation

In the past, giant pandas were hunted for their fur and meat. Even today, panda pelts can fetch more money on the open market than most rural farmers will see in a lifetime. However, education programmes mean that few pandas are now deliberately killed.

It is deforestation that is the primary cause of concern to the future of the species. Giant pandas used to be found in mountain regions throughout Southern and Eastern China, Vietnam and Myanmar. Habitat loss, due to an increase in logging and farming, means that isolated giant panda populations can now be found in only six mountain ranges: the Qinling, Min, Qionglai, Daxiangling, Xiaoxiangling and Liang.

Fortunately, the giant panda's biggest ally in its fight for survival is its fame. The Chinese regard this shy, secretive bear as a national treasure and alternative, ecofriendly forest uses are now being developed to safeguard the panda's habitats. It is still early days, but population numbers appear to have stabilized, and there is hope that this trend will continue.

Giant pandas may spend up to 12 hours a day eating and foraging for food.

An elongated wrist bone on its forepaw helps the panda to grip the bamboo shoots.

Eating the fresh bamboo leaves first, the panda then strips the tough skin from the stem.

Inside the stem is a tender centre, which the panda's giant molars reduces to an edible pulp.

Lion-tailed Macaque

Of the 20 known species of macaque that make their homes in the mountainous forests of Africa and Asia, the lion-tailed is the most striking in appearance, with its long, tufted tail and luxuriant grey-brown 'mane'. It is also one of the rarest.

Key Facts	ORDER *Primates* / FAMILY *Cercopithecidae* GENUS & SPECIES *Macaca silenus*
Weight	Male up to 10kg; female up to 6kg
Length Head and body Tail	46–61cm 25–38cm
Sexual maturity	Male 8 years; female 5 years
Mating season	Year round, although births peak in the rainy seasons
Gestation period	165 days
Number of young	1
Breeding interval	At least 2 years
Typical diet	Fruit, leaves, seeds,grasses; invertebrates and small reptiles
Life span	Female up to 9 years; male not known

Newborn
Unlike adult macaques, newborns lack the distinctive facial hair. This starts to grow after a few months, but the leonine tufts develop only with maturity.

Teeth

The lion-tailed macaque is
an omnivore – it eats both
vegetable and animal foodstuffs.
Its teeth therefore include flat,
grinding molars for chewing
seeds and fruit, and sharp
incisors which are used for
cutting through flesh.

Hands

In common with all primates,
macaques have long, dexterous
fingers and toes, and opposable
thumbs. These enable them to
grip and manipulate objects
with ease.

Comparisons

In common with its smaller lion-tailed cousin, the pig-tailed macaque (*Macata nemestrina*) lives primarily in evergreen forests. Although it is currently listed as 'Vulnerable' on the IUCN's Red List, this brown, stub-tailed monkey is much more widespread than the lion-tailed macaque and can be found from Eastern India to Indonesia. One of the reasons for this may be the fact that it is less reliant on trees and will travel on the forest floor.

Lion–tailed macaque

Pig–tailed macaque

Lion-tailed macaques spend the vast part of their lives in the tree tops. Here they live in close-knit family groups of 10 to 30 individuals, which usually include one or two males. This is a gregarious species, and troops tend to forage together, using trembling 'whoo whoo' cries to keep in touch with one another. Sadly, forests are being cleared throughout India, so this is a sound that has now almost vanished from the continent.

Lion-tailed macaque habitats

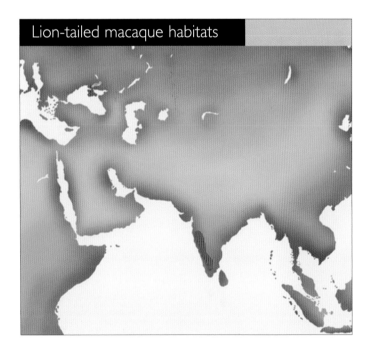

Something Old, Something New

In the system of animal classification called taxonomy, animals are split into groups based on their biological similarities. For every animal, there are seven distinct groupings: kingdom, phylum, class, order, family, genus and species. Aye-ayes, chimpanzees, lemurs, orang-utans and macaques all belong to the order Primates, which is one of the largest and most diverse groups of mammals. Within this order is the suborder Anthropoidea, which includes New World monkeys (family Cebidae), Old World monkeys (family Cercopithecidae), marmosets (Callithricidae) and anthropoid apes (family Pongidae).

Lion-tailed macaques belong to the Old World of Asia, rather than the New World of Central America, where monkeys such as titis and sakis make their home. As well as living in different continents, these two monkey families are physically different, making it easy to identify a New or an Old World inhabitant.

A Monkey's Tail

The dense rainforests that snake through Latin America are home to around 70 species of monkey. These very different New World species share numerous characteristics separating them from their Old World cousins, such as macaques. For example, New World monkeys have 36 teeth. Macaques have 32, which is the same number as humans. Old World monkeys also have their nostrils closer together, have shorter, less 'woolly' fur and have rounder faces than their Latin American relatives. Perhaps the most obvious difference, though, is their tails.

Most primates have dexterous hands and feet, as well as opposable thumbs that are long and flexible enough to touch the other digits. This is especially useful in gripping branches. New World monkeys have poorly developed opposable thumbs. To compensate for this, their tails are prehensile and can be used to grip branches. African and Asian Old World species do not have prehensile tails and so must rely on their hands and feet to do the gripping for them. Some scientists believe that it is this small difference which enabled Old World primates to develop into the type of sophisticated tool user from which humans eventually evolved. Being forced to use their hands made them develop skills that are used by humans today.

Threats and Conservation

Macaque troops are generally unwilling to venture into regions where trees are scarce. For the macaque, trees are not only a source of food and shelter, but also offer safe highways through their range, without the need to travel on the ground. This reliance on trees has made macaques increasingly vulnerable. As forests are cleared to make way for plantations, agriculture, dams and power lines, macaque communities have become isolated. They are nervous of people, who hunt them, which makes troops trapped in surviving enclaves of forest reluctant to leave. The result has been starvation and interbreeding. It is believed that there may be fewer than 400 lion-tailed macaques left in the wild. Captive breeding programmes have been established, but these will be successful only if there are safe and protected areas where the macaques can be released.

A newborn baby macaque takes refuge in the arms of its attentive mother.

As it becomes older, it is able to cling to its mother's belly as she forages for food.

As it grows, the baby macaque switches from clinging to its mother's belly to riding piggyback.

By watching adults carefully, the baby is soon able to learn vital survival skills.

Orang-utan

The word 'orang-utan' comes from the Malay for 'man of the woods', and it is easy to see why this large ape was given such an evocative name. Like all apes, orang-utans are closely related to humans and share many of our traits: intelligence, creativity and sociability. Sadly, these rainforest dwellers are also increasingly rare in the wild.

Face

A male orang-utan's face is broad, with prominent, fleshy check flanges. These are presumably designed to make him more appealing to females.

Arms

When a male orang-utan stretches out his arms, the combined length, from fingertip to fingertip, is longer than his entire body.

Key Facts	ORDER *Primates* / FAMILY *Pongidae* GENUS & SPECIES *Pongo pygmaeus*
Weight	Male 59–91kg (130–201lb); Female 36–50kg (79–110lb
Height	Up to 1.5m (4 ft 11in)
Sexual maturity	Usually 7 years, but male does not breed until 13–15 years old
Breeding season	All year round
Gestation period	233–265 days
Number of young	1
Birth interval	3–4 years; often much longer
Typical diet	Mainly fruit; also leaves, berries and nuts; occasionally small mammals, birds, eggs and invertebrates
Life span	35–40 years or more

Hair

The orang-utan's long, coarse, reddish-brown hair is not only distinctive, but also provides good protection from the rain.

Comparisons

The orang-utan may be up to ten times heavier than the lar gibbon (*Hylobates lar*), but both species are accomplished aerial acrobats. Although slower and more deliberate in its movements than the gibbon, both apes rarely descend to the ground. Instead, they travel through the forest by swinging – arm over arm and from branch to branch – in a motion called 'brachiating'.

Orang-utan

Lar gibbon

There are two subspecies of orang-utan: the Bornean (*Pongo pygmaeus pygmaeus*) and Sumatran (*Pongo pygmaeus abelii*). The Bornean, and its three known subspecies, are all currently listed as 'Endangered', while the Sumatran is 'Critically Endangered' on the IUCN's Red List. In 2004 a population assessment for orang-utans took place, it was estimated that there were about 60,000 orang-utans in the wild. They are disappearing at a rate of 5000 per year which means they will be extinct in the wild in ten years time.

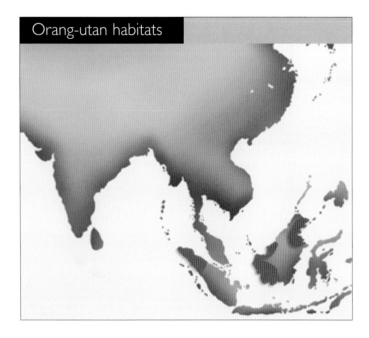

Orang-utan habitats

Monkeys, Apes and Humans

In Africa, the dominant primates are chimpanzees and gorillas. In Asia, this niche has been filled by gibbons and orang-utans. All four of these species belong to the family Pongidae and are classed as anthropoid (or manlike) apes.

Unlike monkeys, apes have several physical characteristics that link them directly to humans. First, in common with humans, they have lost their tails. Secondly, when they walk on two legs, they tend to adopt an upright posture. Even on all fours, true apes do not support their weight on the soles of their feet, like monkeys, but on the outer edge of the foot, like humans. Finally, they have an enlarged cranial capacity. Although size is not everything, having a brain that is large in proportion to your body weight is a good indicator of intelligence. In fact, although orang-utans are generally placed between gorillas and chimpanzees in terms of intelligence, their brain size is comparable to that of a human.

Vive La Difference!

Orang-utans are sexually dimorphic: the males and females of the species are physically quite different from each other. Males are, on average, around twice the size of the females, growing up to 91kg (200lb) in weight and around 1.5m (4ft 11in) in height. In addition to their great size, males also have a prominent, enlarged throat sac. This is used to make the loud roars which advertise their availability to breed to the females, who are receptive all year round. Male orang-utans also have rounded cheek flaps, called pads, on either side of their face. These develop when the orang-utan reaches sexually maturity, which is at about 15 years old. These flashy flanges are probably designed to make them look larger and more aggressive to other male orang-utans, with whom they have to compete for territory and breeding rights.

Threats and Conservation

It would seem logical to assume that such a rapid fall in the numbers of any species must be the result of some catastrophic natural disaster – and this is almost true in the case of the orang-utan. Indonesia's great rainforests (which are second only in size to those in Brazil) are vanishing at the rate of around 2.5 million hectares (6.2 million acres)

every year. This deforestation represents an environmental catastrophe of global proportions, as animal and plant species are lost for ever.

The cause of such large-scale destruction is illegal logging. The local government does have a modest, and potentially sustainable, logging programme, but 73 per cent of all tree-felling in the region happens illegally, to provide plywood and paper for Western consumers. The problem is compounded by the fact that forests are also being cleared to plant palm oil plantations, which provide a valuable income for local people. Even though orang-utans are protected, continued deforestation means that, soon, they could literally have nowhere left to live. Unless illegal logging and farming are controlled, the orang-utan may be extinct by 2010.

Until it is weaned, at around three years old, a baby orang-utan rarely leaves its mother's side.

Orang-utans give birth to one young at a time. With gaps of up to five years between births, this allows them to be attentive mothers.

By sharing food with her baby, the orang-utan mother teaches her child which food is good and safe to eat.

Young female orang-utans usually stay with their mother until another baby is born. They learn vital parenting skills.

Red Panda

Although smaller and less well known than its namesake, the red panda now shares the dubious distinction of being listed with the giant panda as 'Endangered' on the IUCN's Red List. Time, it seems, is running out for these reclusive and gentle tree dwellers.

Key Facts	ORDER *Carnivora* / FAMILY *Ailuropochidae* GENUS & SPECIES *Ailurus fulgens*	
Weight	3–6kg (6.6–13lb)	
Length Head and body	51–63cm (20–25in)	
Sexual maturity	18–20 months	
Mating season	January to March	
Number of young	1 to 4 but usually 2	
Gestation period	90–145 days	
Breeding interval	1 year	
Typical diet	Mainly bamboo shoots, fruit, roots, acorns and grasses, but sometimes insects, eggs, nestlings and small rodents	
Life span	Unknown in wild; up to 14 years in captivity	

Tail

In common with many arboreal species, the red panda has a long tail, which is used to help it to keep its balance when clambering about in the tree tops.

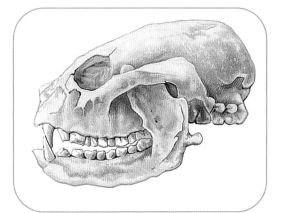

Jaw

A powerful jaw and large grinding molar teeth enable the red panda to turn tough bamboo shoots into an edible pulp. Spike-like canines show that, despite the red panda's predominantly vegetarian diet, it was designed to eat meat.

Feet

The red panda's claws – so useful in helping it to climb trees – can be partly retracted to prevent them becoming blunt when the panda walks.

Red pandas are already extinct in two of the seven Chinese provinces in which they were previously found. Worldwide, species numbers may be as low as 16,000.

What's in a Name?

All animals have a Latin name that enables scientists to clearly identify them. Under this system, called taxonomy, the red panda is known as *Ailurus fulgens.* This means 'fire-coloured cat', and refers to the panda's thick, glossy, reddish fur rather than to any real catlike characteristics. Fortunately, such complex names tend not to be used in everyday life. The preference is for common names, which vary from country to country. In Chinese, for example, this small mammal is called *hunho* meaning 'fire fox'. In Nepal, it is known as the *chitwa* or *wah* because of the distinctive

call that it makes. The name 'panda' was chosen by the naturalist Thomas Hardwicke (1755–1835), who was the first European to encounter the species in 1821. In his writings, he used the Nepalese name *wah*, but also mentioned that locals called it *poonya*, meaning 'eater of bamboo', the food that forms a large part of the red panda's diet. 'Panda' is the anglicized version of *poonya*.

Tree Nurseries

Although male red pandas are naturally solitary by nature, they generally have several females within their territory. As breeding season approaches (between January and March), the males will seek out a female to mate. They then return to their solitary lives. It is left to the females to make the necessary preparations for motherhood. As red

After passing a few hours basking in the tree tops, the red panda goes in search of food.

A bamboo thicket represents an irresistible feast to a hungry red panda.

After his meal, the panda heads for the river, where he scoops up pawfuls of water to drink.

Food and water are worth fighting for, and male pandas will actively defend their territory from intruders.

pandas spend most of their lives in the tree tops, young mums-to-be prepare a special nursery in a tree hollow. This is where they give birth and is the place that will provide protection and shelter for their young. Birth takes place around 130–160 days after mating, with up to five births per litter. These tiny furry babies need all the help they can get, as they are blind for the first few weeks of their life. The bond established between mother and babies during this period is especially strong, and most young will stay with the mother until the next year's litter is born and they are ready to start families of their own.

Threats and Conservation

In captivity, red pandas eat a wide variety of food, from fruit to fresh meat. They are technically carnivores, but in the wild they survive almost exclusively on a diet of bamboo – a form of fibrous grass that grows in tall, hollow stems up to 37m (121ft 5in) in height.

Pandas select only the young, tender growing leaves and shoots, which are higher in nutritional value than older, tougher stems. However, bamboo is still a poor food source: to thrive, an adult red panda must consume around 30 per cent of its body weight every day, and also conserve energy by taking regular tree-top naps. The loss of bamboo forests, to logging and agriculture, has therefore had a devastating effect on red panda numbers. Red pandas also occasionally fall prey to hunters because fur hats, with the

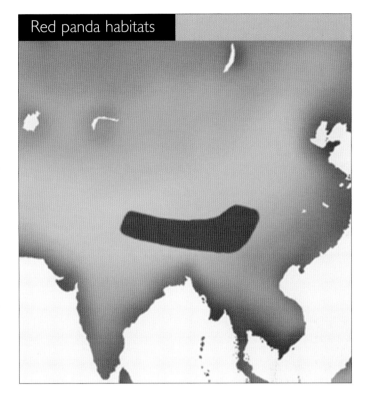

Red panda habitats

panda's long tail hanging down the back, are regarded as lucky talismans by newlyweds in the Yunnan Province. The animals are protected in Nepal and China, but species numbers will start to recover only once habitat loss is halted, too.

Comparisons

For decades, fierce debate has raged about the red panda's true scientific classification. Thanks to its racoon-like appearance, it was, for many years, classified as a member of the family Procyonidae, like the ringtail. Some scientists place in its own family, Ailuridae, while there are still some who argue that it should be listed, along with the giant panda, as a member of the bear family Ursidae.

Red panda

Ringtail

Siberian Tiger

Agile, graceful and beautiful, Siberian tigers are one of Asia's last surviving big predators. Once roaming freely throughout Eastern Siberia, this great feline now occupies isolated regions in some of Asia's most inhospitable terrain.

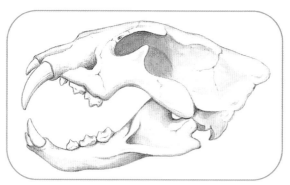

Skull and teeth
A big skull helps to anchor this large cat's powerful jaw muscles firmly in place. Long canines and sharp carnassials complete the tiger's impressive arsenal.

Foot
For many hunters, stealth is the key to success. Soft pads on the Siberian tiger's feet help it to move silently when it is stalking prey.

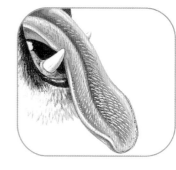

Tongue
Tiny barbs cover the Siberian tiger's tongue, giving it the texture of sandpaper. This rough surface is ideal for scraping flesh from bone.

Key Facts

ORDER *Carnivora* / FAMILY *Felidae* / GENUS & SPECIES *Panthera tigris altaica*

Weight	Male 180–300kg (397–662lb)
	Female 100–165kg (221–364lb)
Length	
Head and body	1.6–2.8m (5ft 3in–9ft 2in)
Tail	60–95cm (24–37in)
Shoulder height	1–1.1m (3ft 3in–3ft 7in)
Sexual maturity	Male 4–5 years; female 3–4 years
Mating season	November–April
Gestation period	104–106 days
Number of young	1–6 (usually 2 or 3)
Birth interval	2–2.5 years
Typical diet	Pigs, deer, bears, small birds and fish
Life span	15 years in the wild; up to 26 in captivity

Siberian tiger habitats

The Siberian tiger is also known as the Amur, Manchurian, Ussurian and North-East China tiger.

Wrap up Warm

There are five tiger subspecies – the Bengal, Indo-Chinese, Siberian, South China and Sumatran. Of these, the Siberian is the largest, growing up to 3.3m (10ft 10in) from head to tail. Although we generally think of these big cats as tropical inhabitants, it is believed that all the world's tiger subspecies are descended from the Siberian.

Spreading out across Europe and Asia during the Ice Age, their ancient ancestors quickly established themselves as top cat in a range of environments. As they moved from snowbound tundra to rainforest, this original Siberian model slowly evolved to suit a range of new environments and climates. In the frozen north, keeping warm is a major concern, so this graceful predator has a long coat and an extra layer of body fat to keep out the harsh elements. Its Indian relative, the Bengal tiger, has much shorter hair, making it better suited to a life in a warmer climate.

All Alone

The Siberian tiger is a beleaguered creature. It is mostly found in eastern Asiatic Russia, in the Amur-Ussuri region of Primorye and Khabarovsk. A small number (about 10 per cent of the total) are across the border in China and another pocket, of unknown size, is in North Korea. Most Siberian tigers inhabit coniferous, oak and birch woodlands, but even here prey is scarce and the weather extreme. To survive, these hardy cats must cover vast territories – up to 1000 square kilometres (386 square miles). An adult tiger needs around 9kg (20lb) of meat a day just to provide its body with enough fuel to keep

Comparisons

The puma (*Puma concolor*) is the New World's biggest feline predator. Although around two-thirds of the average size of a Siberian tiger, this compact cat shares much of its relative's natural acrobatic agility. Able to jump 4.5m (14ft 9in) from a standing start, and over 13m (45ft) when running, it makes a powerful and formidable hunter.

Siberian tiger   Puma

warm. The bulk of this is provided by elk and wild boar, but the tiger is an adaptable species and will eat anything from small mammals to carrion. As only one in ten hunting trips is successful, tigers tend to gorge themselves when they do eat, consuming as much as 40kg (88lb) of meat in one sitting. For the females, the problems of survival are intensified during the breeding season. This is the only time that adult tigers spend time together. After mating, the male goes back to his solitary hunt, leaving the female to raise her cubs alone. Not surprisingly, cub mortality rates are high.

Threats and Conservation

Throughout the twentieth century numbers of Siberian tigers have dwindled and today only about 2300 remain.

This is despite the fact that these iconic cats have been legally protected in Russia since 1992. There are now three protected areas in the region, where tigers are considered safe from poachers and human encroachment – the Sikhote-Alin, Lazovsky and Kedrovaya Pad reserves. There is also legislation to stop illegal hunting and the trade in tiger body parts, but, as ever, such laws are hard to enforce in remote regions.

Increasingly, the future of this species relies not on its wild population, but on the 500 Siberian tigers living in zoos around the world. This population is the result of one of the world's longest established captive breeding programmes. Descended from just 83 wild cats, these captive tigers represent a diverse and stable gene pool, and it is hoped that they can at some point be released into the wild.

Mating takes place in the winter. After a four-month gestation period, two or three cubs are born in a secluded spot.

Grabbing the loose skin at the back of the neck, the mother is able to transport her cubs quickly and safely around her territory.

It can take up to six months before cubs are fully weaned, but they start to eat their first solid food at two months.

If the cubs survive the conditions, they will stay with their mother until they can hunt for themselves at two years old.

Snow Leopard

This rare and beautiful cat has long been hunted for its thick, silvery coat, which is valued by fur traders. Today, just a few thousand of these agile and skilled predators remain — isolated in the upland steppes and coniferous scrublands of their mountain homelands.

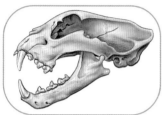

Jaws
With muscular jaws anchored to a large skull, the snow leopard is able to bite down on its prey with incredible force.

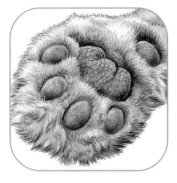

Paws

To help the leopard to maintain its body heat, the soles of its paws are padded with a thick layer of insulating fur.

Key Facts

ORDER *Carnivora* / FAMILY *Felidae* / GENUS & SPECIES *Panthera uncia*

Weight	35–55kg (77–121lb)
Length Head and body Tail	1–1.3m (39–51in) 0.8–1m (31–39in)
Shoulder height	60cm (24in)
Sexual maturity	2–3 years
Mating season	January–April
Gestation period	90–103 days
Number of young	1 to 5, but usually 2 or 3
Birth interval	More than 2 years
Typical diet	Mammals and birds
Life span	Up to 20 years

Snow leopards – or ounces, as they are also called – are often classed as part of the genus *Panthera*. This is the same group to which tigers, jaguars and other leopards belong. Despite similar rosette markings on their coats, however, the snow leopard is actually a member of a separate species called *Uncia uncia*.

Food for Survival

Snow leopards are primarily mountain dwellers. In the summer, they are usually found at 2000–4000m (6561–13,123ft) above sea level, preferring the rocky mountain passes, high valleys and coniferous scrublands where prey such as wild sheep, goats and ibex graze. In the winter, they follow the migrating prey to the warmer lowland forests and grass lands. Leopards are opportunists and will eat almost anything, from small birds to large ungulates (hoofed animals), and they are quite capable of bringing down animals three times their size. Typically, these agile cats are solitary hunters, but a mating pair will often work together to double the odds of a successful kill. After cubs are born – in spring, when food is more abundant – they are completely reliant on their mother for food. It takes three months before they are old enough to accompany her on the hunt and begin to learn vital survival skills for themselves.

The Call of the Wild

The species to which the snow leopard belongs is believed to form a bridge between the big cats of the wild and our

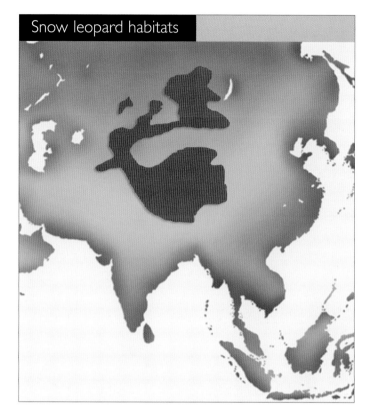

Snow leopard habitats

smaller domestic companions. Snow leopards grow to around 1.3m (4ft 3in) from head to tail, making them the same size as Indian leopards (*Panthera pardus*), but smaller than jaguars and much smaller than lions and tigers. Their heads are small and more rounded than those of the bigger predators. Their legs, too, are short compared to their body

Comparisons

Snow leopard

Clouded leopard

One look at the clouded leopard (*Neofelis nebulosa*) tells us this is a forest inhabitant – it has short limbs, a low body and a long tail, which enables it to climb and keep its balance in the trees. Like the snow leopard, this attractive cat is fast disappearing from its natural habitats in South-East Asia, due to poaching and trapping.

size. The most noticeable difference between snow leopards and other 'big cats' is how they sound. *Panthera* species have a flexible bone at the base of their tongue, which is called a hyoid and which allows them to emit a deep throaty roar. Domestic cats, have a rigid hyoid, so they cannot roar. Snow leopards have an elastic hyoid but they do not roar either, instead, they make quiet 'chuffing' sounds when greeting an old friend.

Threats and Conservation

Most of the animal fur sold in reputable stores comes from mink. This is farmed legally. Yet rare species such as snow leopards are still hunted – illegally – for their fur because it is an expensive (and therefore desirable) commodity. Snow leopard bones, too, are still used in many traditional Chinese medicines, despite the severe penalties for anyone found trading in them. The problem for the authorities is that snow leopards live in areas that are difficult to police and poor. It can be hard to convince a farmer struggling to feed his family that a valuable snow leopard is worth more alive than dead. Even in areas where leopards are protected, their traditional prey is becoming scarce, which puts pressure on surviving populations.

The future lies in the hands of the Snow Leopard Survival Program. This involves conservation groups and zoos worldwide, and the hope is that numbers of snow leopards can be built up in captivity, until the day that it is safe to release them into a protected wild environment.

Camouflaged among the rocks, the snow leopard lies in wait for a grazing markhor.

Able to leap up to 10m (33ft) horizontally, the leopard can easily catch its prey unawares.

The prey is killed quickly, with a bite to the throat from its huge jaws.

During the breeding season, mother and hungry cubs will share the kill with the male.

Sumatran Rhino

Sumatran rhinoceroses are the smallest known species of rhino. With their covering of coarse red hair and double horns, they are also one of the most unusual. Solitary and secretive, these pygmy rhinos are now an increasingly rare sight in the upland forests of their island home.

Skull

The Sumatran rhinoceros's skull is large and heavy. The bony, noselike growth at the tip of the skull is the growing point for the rhino's distinctive horns.

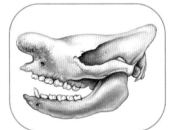

Key Facts	ORDER *Perissodactyla* FAMILY *Rhinocerotidae* GENUS & SPECIES *Dicerorhinus sumatrensis*
Weight	600–1000kg (0.6–0.9 tons)
Length Head and body	2.2–3m (7ft 2in–9ft 8in)
Shoulder height	1.1–1.5m (3ft 7in–4ft 11in)
Sexual maturity	7–8 years
Mating season	Unknown, birth peaks in October–May
Gestation period	Unknown, probably about 18 months
Number of young	1
Birth interval	3–4 years
Typical diet	Saplings, leaves, fruit and twigs
Life span	More than 32 years in captivity

Forefeet

At the end of strong, columnar legs, the rhino's forefeet have three toes, each of which carries a nail-like hoof.

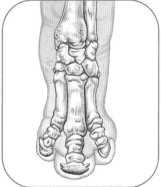

Comparisons

Like the Sumatran rhinoceros, the Javan rhino (*Rhinoceros sondaicus*) is listed as 'Critically Endangered' by the IUCN. Unfortunately, with fewer than 60 individuals left, there is little hope that this large, hairless forest dweller will continue to survive in the wild.

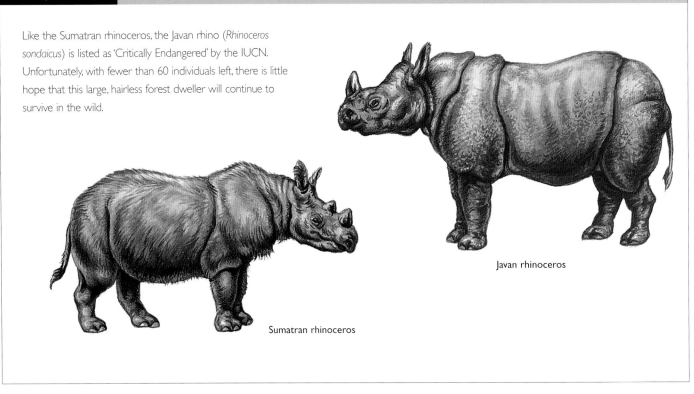

Javan rhinoceros

Sumatran rhinoceros

This small, barrel-chested member of the family Rhinocerotidae was once common throughout Asia, from the Himalayas to Vietnam. Now fewer than 300 may survive in the wild.

Sumatran rhino habitats

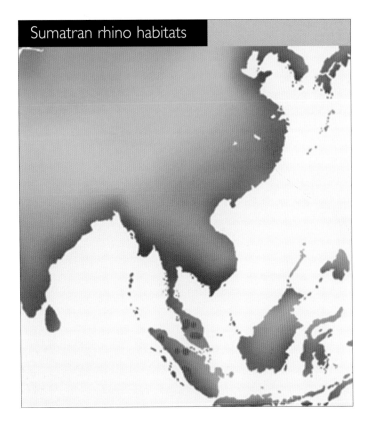

Horns and Hair

The name 'rhinoceros' comes from the Greek for 'nose' (*rhino*) and 'horn' (*keras*), and is a reference to the curious spikes that grow in the middle of this stocky mammal's snout, like huge upturned teeth. Unlike teeth, these spikes are not made from enamel, but comprise a mass of matted, hairlike material called keratin. These impressive protuberances are not actually horns, although they appear to be. True horns, such as those grown by deer, are solid and embedded in the skull. A rhino's spikes are hollow at the base and embedded in the skin.

Perhaps the most impressive horns of the family belong to the white rhinoceros (*Ceratotherium simum*), whose large anterior spike can grow to a recorded 157.5cm (62in). Typically, African rhinos have two horns and Indian rhinos have one, but the Sumatran is the exception to the rule. This furry pygmy has two small horns, one at the tip of its snout and one just above the eyes. The larger of these grows to just 90cm (36in) and the other can be so small that it is virtually invisible. These are little use for fighting, but instead make a handy tool when foraging for food.

Salt Licks and Mud Baths

Sumatran rhinoceroses are crepuscular and nocturnal: they are most active just before dawn and after sunset. It is then that they begin to forage for food. Typically, Sumatran rhinos live in lightly forested hills and make good use of the available resources. Even this small species needs to consume around 40kg (88lb) of food a day to stay healthy, so leaves, twigs, fruit and roots are all on the menu. They also need to supplement their diet with minerals such as calcium and sodium, which they obtain by either ingesting soil or licking specific rocks. These 'salt licks' are vital to the rhino's health, and it is believed that every male's territory contains at least one.

Another regular feature of a rhino's range is a mud wallow. During the day, rhinos like to unwind in a relaxing mud bath or shallow pool. Such wallows are made by the rhino and are part of their personal grooming routine. Rhinos have no sweat glands, so the mud not only helps to keep them cool, but it helps to keep their skin free from parasites, too.

Threats and Conservation

Sumatran rhinoceroses are the last survivors of an ancient family whose ancestors included the woolly rhinoceros, which vanished from our planet 10,000 years ago. Just ten years ago, it looked like the Sumatran rhino was about to join its long extinct relative. Numbers of surviving wild rhinos had fallen by an estimated 50 per cent and the species was listed as 'Critically Endangered' on the IUCN's Red List. The international community reacted quickly and concerted efforts were made to save this mammal. Moves included global cooperation to prevent poaching and the sale of rhino parts, which are highly valued in Chinese medicine. Captive breeding programmes were also established. It is still too soon to be sure if the Sumatran rhinoceros has a future, but there is real hope of success.

The shade of a tree or a long mud wallow helps to keep the rhino cool during the day.

As the sun sets, the rhino sets out to find a salt lick, which provides it with vital minerals it needs in its diet.

Finding a small tree, the rhino uses its bulk to bend back the trunk and reach the young leaves at the top of the branches.

Chewing helps to break up the vegetation into an easily digestible pulp.

Bengal Tiger

The power, grace and beauty of this great cat has been its downfall. For centuries, hunters have sought to prove their skill by pitting themselves against this ultimate predator. Such unequal contests – guns versus claws – have sent tiger numbers plummeting. Now legally protected, Bengal tigers must face new challenges if they are to survive in the wild.

Teeth
The tiger's long canine teeth are designed to stab down into its prey's flesh and rip it apart with ease.

Key Facts	ORDER *Carnivora* / FAMILY *Felidae* GENUS & SPECIES *Panthera tigris tigris*	
Weight	180–265kg (397–584lb)	
Length Head and body Tail	1.9–2.2m (6ft 3in–7ft 3in) 80–90cm (31–35in)	
Shoulder height	90–95cm (35–37in)	
Sexual maturity	Female 3–4 years; male 4–5 years	
Mating season	Winter to spring	
Gestation period	95–112 days	
Number of young	2–4	
Typical diet	Sambar deer, chital deer, buffalo, wild pigs, gaur and monkeys	
Life span	10–15 years but can live up to 26 years in the wild	

Coat

The seemingly bold combination of orange and black stripes is a form of natural camouflage that breaks up the outline of the tiger's body and helps it to hide from both predators and prey.

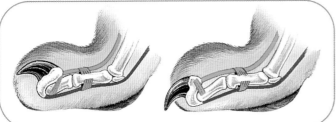

Claws

In common with most cats, a tiger's claws retract when not in use. This prevents them from becoming blunt as the tiger walks.

Comparisons

The Siberian tiger is both larger and heavier than its Bengali relative. With a long coat to keep it warm in the cool northern climate, this huge, shaggy cat is now found mainly in Eastern Russia.

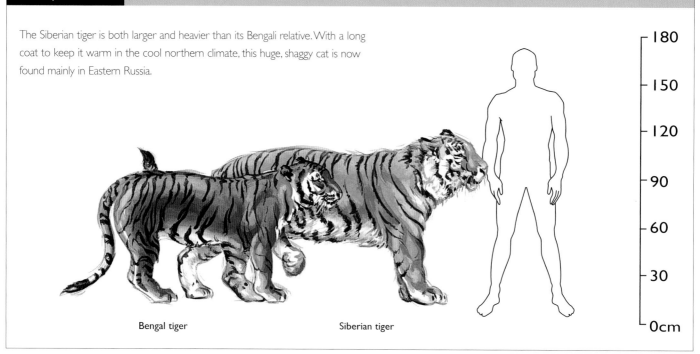

Bengal tiger   Siberian tiger

180
150
120
90
60
30
0cm

Worldwide, there are only five remaining tiger subspecies: the Bengal (*Panthera tigris tigris*), Sumatran (*Panthera tigris sumatrae*), South China (*Panthera tigris amoyensis*), Indochinese (*Panthera tigris corbetti*) and Amur or Siberian (*Panthera tigris altaica*). All are listed as either 'Endangered' or 'Critically Endangered'on the IUCN's Red List.

Coats of Many Colours

The Bengal tiger is the archetypal tiger, with a large, muscular body covered in orange and black stripes. Like human fingerprints, a tiger's coat is unique, and each of these distinctive stripes varies in length, width, spacing and colour. The darkest of all tigers are the Sumatran, whose coat is covered with broad, closely spaced single or doubled black stripes. Siberian tigers, which range from birch woodlands to the barren wastes of Siberia, are much paler, with less obvious stripes and a white belly. This provides ideal camouflage in the regions that it roams. The most striking of all of these great cats is probably the white tiger, which has a totally white coat, covered in pale brown stripes. It also has blue rather than yellow eyes. Despite their unique appearance, white tigers are not a separate subspecies, but a rare variant of the Bengal Tiger, and they are usually found only in zoos.

Big Cats, Little Cats

Tigers are the largest members of the family Felidae – the same group to which domestic cats belong. In common with all felines, these big cats are skilled hunters whose

reputation relies on their strength, agility and speed. The largest of these great cats is the Siberian tiger. A fully grown male Siberian tiger can be up to 3.3m (10ft 9in) from head to tail, but there is quite a lot of variation between the subspecies. A male Sumatran tiger, for example, is the smallest of all the tigers and may reach only 2.4m (7ft 10in) head to tail. In India, Bengal tigers are among one of the largest predators.

Bengal tiger habitats

Bengal tigers are muscular hunters which have long had a reputation as 'man-eaters'. It is true that frightened, sick or injured tigers have been known to attack humans, but most actively avoid any contact with man. Their preferred food is wild deer, pigs and cattle, but they are not fussy eaters and will make a meal of anything from carrion to small reptiles and even fish. The scarcity of wildlife in some regions has, unfortunately, led tigers into conflict with humans because they will raid farms for food when nothing else is available.

Threats and Conservation

Of the world's remaining tiger subspecies, the South China is the rarest, with possibly fewer than 80 individuals left in the wild. This compares to around 250 mature Sumatran and Siberian tigers, 1700 Indochinese and up to 4000 Bengal tigers. When we consider that these elegant hunters were once a common sight from Turkey through to Siberia, such low numbers are shocking. Yet, considering the abuse suffered by tigers for centuries, it is fortunate that any have survived at all.

Although tigers are now protected in the wild and this is a positive step, their continued survival remains hanging by a thread – especially in regions where any legal threats are outweighed by the financial rewards to be gained from selling tiger skins and bones, which are used in medicines. Loss of habitat and a decline in the tiger's traditional prey species has also decimated population numbers. The future of this beautiful cat depends increasingly on captive breeding programmes and international cooperation to establish secure and protected reserves. In India, which has bred Bengal tigers in captivity since 1880, the future is hopeful. For the South China Tiger, though, time may have already run out.

Hunting at night, the tiger stalks its prey, using the long grass to stay out of sight.

Covering the distance between itself and its prey in a few powerful bounds, the tiger attacks.

The tiger uses its claws to grab its prey and pull it down to the ground.

Once dead, the tiger drags its prey's carcass to a hidden spot so that it can eat undisturbed.

PHILIPPINES

INDONESIA

PAPUA NEW
GUINEA

AUSTRALIA

Great
Sandy
Desert

Tanami
Desert

Simpson
Desert

Great Victoria
Desert

Darling Range

Great Dividing Range

Tasmania

SOUTH PACIFIC
OCEAN

SOUTHERN
OCEAN

NEW
ZEALAND

Australasia

Australasia is comprised of Australia, New Zealand, Papua New Guinea and its neighbouring islands. For much of its history, this vibrant region was isolated from the rest of the world, allowing its flora and fauna to flourish undisturbed. Today, much of this unique plant and animal life is vanishing.

For rural island nations such as Papua New Guinea, the problems faced by its wildlife are familiar ones: overhunting and loss of land to farming and industry as the region develops. In Australia and New Zealand, the situation is more complex. Both these nations have well-established economies. Most of their population live in the cities and never come into direct contact with wildlife – but their presence can be felt everywhere. Land use has changed, pollution has increased and new species have been introduced. European cattle, sheep and deer now complete for resources with native species. Dogs, cats, foxes, rabbits and (inadvertently) rats have been brought to the continent, too. On islands such as New Zealand, the effect has been devastating. There are currently 128 species listed as 'Critically Endangered', 'Endangered' or 'Vulnerable' in New Zealand, and a staggering 565 in Australia.

Public awareness of the problems facing Australasia's wildlife is high. A scientist once said that: 'Examining Australia's wildlife is like working on another planet.' In the past, it was these differences that made the region's wildlife so vulnerable. Today, it is what attracts attention, and this may yet prove to be their salvation.

Double-wattled Cassowary

Standing up to 1.7m (5ft 7in) tall, the huge double-wattled cassowary is just one of Australia's many species of large flightless birds that are now threatened with extinction.

Juvenile
A cassowary develops its striking back plumage only once it reaches adulthood, which is at around three years of age.

Wattles
Two loose folds of red, yellow, blue or purple skin hang down from the cassowary's throat – giving them their common name. These folds tend to be brighter in females, but their purpose is unknown.

Key Facts

ORDER *Casuariiformes* / FAMILY *Casuariidae* / GENUS & SPECIES *Casuarius casuarius*

Weight	Male 29–45kg (64–99lb); Female 58kg (128lb)
Length	1.3–1.7m (4ft 3in–5ft 6in)
Sexual maturity	3 or 4 years
Breeding season	June–October
Number of eggs	3–5
Incubation period	About 50 days
Fledging period	About 36 weeks
Breeding interval	Probably 1 year
Typical diet	Fallen fruit; also fungi, insects, snails, small mammals and birds; occasionally carrion
Life span	At least 12–19 years

Plumage
Long, coarse feathers form
a thick cloak around the
cassowary's body. These protect
it from the weather as well as
from potentially hazardous
undergrowth.

Legs and feet
The cassowary's powerful legs
are covered with scales, not
skin. Its feet are tipped with
three extremely long, sharp
claws. The claw on the second
toe can grow to 12cm (4.7in)
and is useful for defence.

Double-wattled cassowary habitats

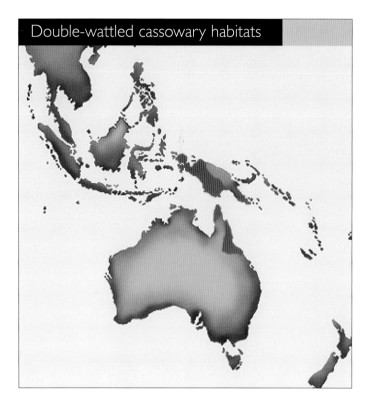

There are two bird families which make up the order Casuariformes. The first is the family Dromaiidae, to which the emu belongs. The second is the family Casuariidae, to which three species of cassowary belong: the southern or double-wattled cassowary (*Casuarius casuarius*), the larger northern or single-wattled cassowary (*Casuarius unappendiculatus*) and the dwarf or Bennett's cassowary (*Casuarius bennetti*).

Big Birds

The double-wattled cassowary is a startling sight. This enormous bird gets its name from the two folds of bright red- or yellow-coloured skin that hang from its it blue neck. These folds are present in two of the three species of cassowary and are probably designed to help it attract a mate. In direct contrast to these vibrant wattles are the cassowary's long, black feathers. Cassowaries cannot fly, so they do not need to have feathers that are smooth and sleek. Instead, they grow like thick fur, and help to protect it from the weather and potentially hazardous undergrowth.

It is on this big bird's head that its other most prominent feature can be found – the brown, bonelike 'casque'. It has been suggested that this is used to dig for food, but it may also play an important role in mating, as the casque continues to grow throughout the bird's life and shows that that the bird has reached a certain level of maturity and dominance.

Father's Day

Cassowaries mate during the dry weather, from June to October. It is then that food is more plentiful, so both the male and female can be in top condition. Usually a solitary male will approach the female to begin the mating ritual. As cassowary females are larger than males, he must be cautious, circling the female and emitting a low booming call until she is ready to receive him. After mating, the couple will stay together until the eggs are laid. Up to five are laid at one time in a makeshift hole in the ground, which the male lines with leaves. Once the eggs are laid, the female then goes off in search of another mate. It is

Comparisons

Dwarf Cassowaries are extremely aggressive, even more than the larger Southern and Northern varieties of the species. In fact, they're one of the few birds that can kill a human, using their powerful legs and long, razor sharp claws to inflict terrible wounds. Fortunately, they live in fairly isolated mountain regions of Papua Guinea.

Dwarf cassowary

Double-wattled cassowary

the father who is left holding the baby, incubating the eggs for around 50 days, until the brown striped chicks are hatched. It takes a further nine months until the chicks are ready for a life on their own. Until that time, the father feeds them, protects them and teaches them everything that they need to know to survive in the adult world.

Threats and Conservation

The double-wattled cassowary is one of the world's largest living birds. Only the African ostrich, which can grow to 2.5m (8ft 2in) in height, is larger. However, both species pale in comparison to New Zealand's moa, which was hunted to extinction soon after Maori settlers arrived on the islands, 1000 years ago. The largest known moas grew to around 4m (13ft 1in), which is the same size as the Madagascan elephant bird. Despite its size, it, too, was hunted to extinction around AD 900, when people settled the region.

What history tells us is that extinction is nothing new, especially when people move into previously uninhabited regions and disturb nature's natural balance. However, it is the speed with which birds such as the cassowary are vanishing that worries conservationists. The numbers of southern cassowary have fallen by 30 per cent in the past ten years, and the species is listed as 'Vulnerable' by the IUCN. Habitat destruction has now been halted in Australia, but hunting and loss of habitat continue to be a problem for species in Indonesia and Papua New Guinea.

A cassowary crashes through the thick undergrowth, protected from harm by its heavy feathers and casque.

The cassowary has a varied diet and will eat almost anything, from fruit and leaves to grubs and even fish.

Fast on its feet, the cassowary is easily able to run down and consume the fleeing rat.

Its powerful bill enables it to break open a eat the sweet flesh inside.

Huon Tree Kangaroo

One of the most striking and unusual of all the marsupials, the
Huon tree kangaroo makes its homes in the trees of Papua
New Guinea. This agile and attractive kangaroo is a
popular sight in many of the world's zoos.
In the wild, though, it is rarely seen.

Ears
The inside of a tree kangaroo's
small, rounded ears are lined
with fur. This helps it to keep
out parasites.

Key Facts	ORDER *Diprodontia* / FAMILY *Macropodidae* / GENUS & SPECIES *Dendrolagus matschiei*
Weight	6–9.5kg (13–21lb)
Length Head and body Tail	61–68cm (24–27in) 51–68cm (20–27in)
Sexual maturity	About 2 years
Mating season	Any time of year
Gestation period	32 days
Time in pouch	End of wet season
Number of young	1
Birth interval	About 13 months
Typical diet	Ferns, fruit and leaves; occasionally eats meat
Life span	14 years or more in captivity

Claws

The long, sharp claws found on this arboreal kangaroo not only help it to keep its grip when climbing, but they also make very effective weapons.

On the ground, tree kangaroos hop or walk on all fours, although they appear to be slow and clumsy.

Trees are their natural element. Using its front legs to grip the trunk, the kangaroo propels itself up the tree by using its hind legs.

The tree kangaroo's long tail helps it to keep its balance as it walks along the tree's branches.

Despite its odd appearance, the tree kangaroo is an agile climber, more at home in the branches than the ground.

With its bright, mahogany-coloured coat and chestnut and yellow face markings, the Huon tree kangaroo is one of the most brilliantly coloured of all marsupials.

Weird and Wonderful

When Europeans arrived in Australia and began to investigate the wildlife, they were amazed by what they found. The animals were so curious, and so unlike anything known in Europe, that experts thought that the specimens they had received were fakes, made up from the bodies of lots of different animals all patched together. And is it any wonder? Kangaroos are in themselves extraordinary: a furry animal, with a deerlike head, pointed snout, massive tail and huge hind legs, which they use to jump around the landscape. Now, add more fur, claws for

climbing, and adapt the tail for grasping branches, and you have a tree kangaroo. Although it is much smaller than the ground-dwelling kangaroo, which can grow to 2m (6ft 6in), the tree kangaroo is no less remarkable. Slow and clumsy on the ground, these amazing marsupials are surprisingly agile in trees, and have been known to jump 9m (29ft 6in) from tree to tree.

Down and Up Again

Tree kangaroos belong to the family Macropodidae, which is the same group as ground kangaroos and wallabies. The common ancestor of all these animals is believed to have been a small arboreal marsupial that resembled a modern-day possum. At some point, the two species diverged, when a group of these tree dwellers decided that life was

Comparisons

The Huon tree kangaroo is also known as Matschie's tree kangaroo, after the German zoologist Paul Matschie (1861–1926), who first identified the species. There are around ten other species of tree kangaroos in the world, six of which can be found only in Papua New Guinea. Of these, around half are currently listed as 'Vulnerable' or 'Endangered'.

Grizzled tree kangaroo   Huon tree kangaroo   Doria's tree kangaroo

more pleasant on the ground. All animals adapt to their environment, but changes happen slowly. It may have taken many thousands of years for these small marsupials to develop the powerful hind legs and long counter-balancing tail that enable them to move rapidly over scrubland. But the ultimate result was the kangaroo, and the design was so effective that currently 56 species can be found, from the desert to wetlands. Some even eventually returned to the trees.

Threats and Conservation

Home for the Huon tree kangaroo is on the lower slopes of the Huon Peninsula in Papua New Guinea, a mountainous, tropical island just north of Australia. In recent years, as the population has grown and the international market for wood has boomed, widescale forest clearance has taken place on the island. The lower slopes of the Huon Peninsula – the tree kangaroo's traditional habitat – have already been largely cleared, which has resulted in a 50 per cent fall in tree kangaroo numbers in just ten years. Tree kangaroos are also hunted by local tribes for food, as they are one of the few large mammals on the island.

Huon tree kangaroos are endemic to the Huon Peninsula. They are found virtually nowhere else, which makes them especially vulnerable when land is cleared. Papua New Guinea is unusual in that 97 per cent of the land is owned by the local people. This means that the population, not the government, makes the decisions about

land use. A Tree Kangaroo Conservation Programme has been established to educate locals about the value of biodiversity, and 40,470ha (100,000 acres) have been set aside as a conservation 'corridor'. The kangaroo's long-term future, however, lies in the hands of the Papua New Guineans themselves.

Huon Tree Kangaroo habitats

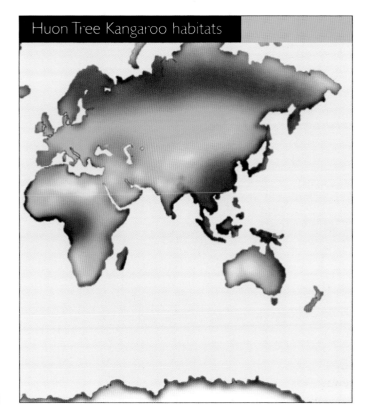

Kakapo

The kakapo is unique. Not only is it the world's biggest parrot, but it also has the distinction of being the world's only nocturnal, flightless parrot. These remarkable birds are listed as 'Critically Endangered', and there are now so few left in the wild that they have all been individually named.

Key Facts	ORDER *Psittaciformes* / FAMILY *Psittacidae* GENUS & SPECIES *Strigops habroptilus*
Weight	Male 2.5kg (5.5lb); female 2kg (4.4lb)
Length	63cm (24.8in)
Sexual maturity	6–8 years
Breeding season	December–May
Number of eggs	2 to 4
Incubation period	30 days
Fledging period	10–12 weeks
Breeding interval	3–5 years; 'relocated' birds breed more frequently
Typical diet	Fruits, seeds, leaves, stems and roots
Life span	60 years or more

Wings
The kakapo cannot fly, but it does occasionally use its wings to slow its descent when it falls from trees.

Bill

The kakapo is a fussy eater. It uses its sharp bill to tear through plants, seeds or fruit, stripping away the best bits to leave little telltale balls of indigestible vegetation behind.

Kakapos are the only members of the genus *Strigops*. Due to the dishlike depressions around their eyes, they were once believed to be members of the owl family, which is where they get their scientific name, *Strigops habroptilus*, meaning 'owl-faced soft feathers'.

Pretty Polly

Most parrots are sociable and roost in huge flocks. Kakapos are generally solitary, although conservation workers have reported that they seem to enjoy the company of humans. Each kakapo has its own territory, which covers up to 0.5 square kilometres (0.3 square miles). It is here that they spend much of the day, hidden from sight in the undergrowth. At night, they come out to feed, clambering around in the tree tops, where they use their wings to help them to keep their balance. These appealing, round-bodied birds can be surprisingly agile on the ground, too. The kakapo's soft, moss-green plumage is little use for flying. Instead, it has developed strong legs. As the kakapo is mainly vegetarian, it does not need to run to pursue prey, but it can walk, with an almost comical, rolling gait, at surprising speeds.

Holding Court

Kakapos live for around 60 years, and are in no hurry to breed. A male does not reach sexual maturity until it is around five years of age. A female waits even longer – between nine and eleven years. When they do mate, the procedure is remarkably complex.

Kakapos are the only parrots in the world that have a 'lek' breeding system. During the mating season, males will leave their traditional territories and head for hilltop

The kakapo uses a depression in the ground as an amphitheatre from which to make his booming mating calls.

Once a female is near, the male performs a courtship display, which he hopes will be more impressive than that of his rivals.

After mating, the female builds a nest and lays one to four eggs, which she incubates diligently.

Until the chicks are ready to leave the nest, they rely on their mother to bring them food.

Comparisons

Keas (*Nestor notabilis*) are able fliers, but they often travel on the ground, where they are mistaken for kakapos. It is their beaks that help us to separate the two species. Kakapos have short, blunt beaks surrounded by sensitive whiskers. Keas have sharp hooked beaks, which they use to tear at animal carcasses and dig up grubs.

Kakapo   Kea

ranges, where they establish their own mating courts. Competition during this time is fierce, and males are often injured as they fight to secure the best sites in the lek, or arena. Once established, the male digs himself a mini amphitheatre. Sitting inside, he emits a series of low-frequency booms, which travel at least 1000m (1093yd) into the bush. He may 'boom' for eight hours a night, until he finally attracts a willing mate. Males can lose up to half their body weight during this exhausting performance and so need lots of high-protein food to fuel their efforts. They therefore cannot mate every year, but wait for high-yielding trees such as the rimu and kahikatea to fruit, which happens only every few years.

Threats and Conservation
When a kakapo is faced with a predator, it stands stock still, relying on its moss-green plumage to help it blend in with the environment. This was a strategy that used to work well against its main predator, the harpagornis eagle (*Harpagornis moorei*), which is now extinct. However, it is useless against mammals – particularly dogs, which can easily track the kakapo by its distinctive honey-like odour. Hunting and loss of habitat have affected kakapo numbers, but it is introduced species that present the greatest threat to their continued survival.

As early as 1891, scientists had realized the dangers to native wildlife from introduced species, and relocated kakapos to Resolution Island, which was free of predators. The kakapos thrived there until 1900, when a handful of stoats swam over to the island and wiped out the entire population in under six years. Today, the remaining

kakapos live on a knife's edge. Surviving populations have been moved to predator-free islands, and these individuals must be relocated regularly to avoid interbreeding, and to give each bird the best chance of survival. They also receive dietary supplements to encourage breeding in years when food is scarce. So far, numbers are stable, but the kakapos could be wiped out should just a few predators find their way onto the islands.

Kakapo habitats

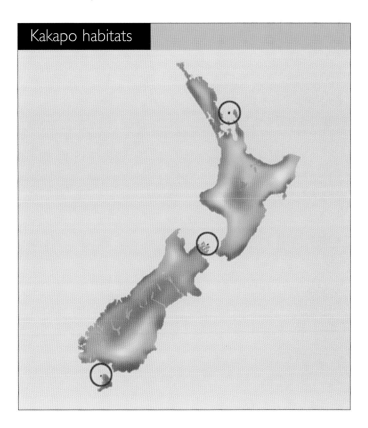

Kiwi

These rare birds are the survivors of a diminished order of 'ratite' (flightless) bird, which includes cassowaries, kakapos, takahes and wekas. With no wings and a long, snoutlike bill, this small, nocturnal species is often referred to as New Zealand's 'honorary mammal'.

Bill

The female kiwi's bill is generally up to one-third longer than the male's. This enables her to search for food in areas where the male cannot reach, doubling the food resources that are available to the couple.

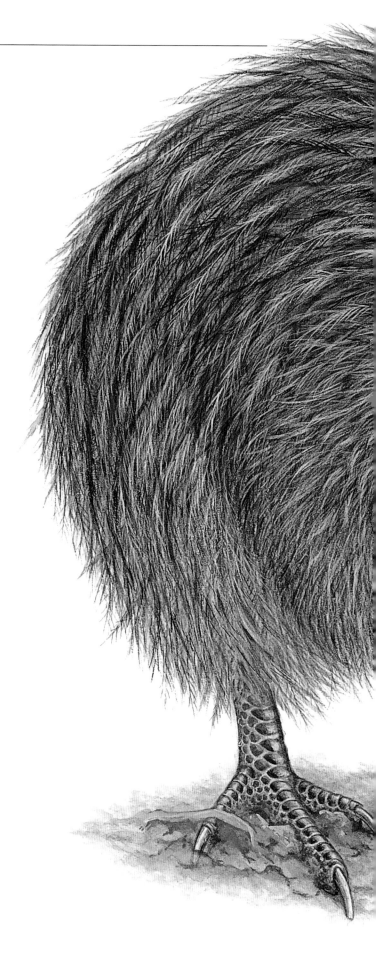

Key Facts	ORDER *Struthioniformes* FAMILY *Apterygidae* GENUS & SPECIES *Apteryx*
Weight	2–8lb (1–3.5kg)
Length	35–65cm (14–26in)
Sexual maturity	2 years
Mating season	August–January
Gestation period	9 months, plus 3 months delayed implantation
Number of young	1 or 2
Birth interval	1 year
Typical diet	Insects, worms and berries
Life span	Unknown in the wild; 30 years in captivity

Legs and feet

Being flightless, the kiwi has powerful legs, which enable it to run away from predators. Its clawed feet are also useful defensive tools, but are more often used to dig in the dirt for insects and grubs.

Nostrils

The kiwi is unique in the bird world, as it has its nostrils at the tip of its bill. This enables the kiwi to sniff for food in the undergrowth.

Kiwi habitats

New Zealand is home to three species of kiwi with several recognised subgroups.

Is it a Bird ...?

New Zealand has no native land mammals, and birds have moved in to take advantage of this. Kiwis have become so well adapted to this new lifestyle that they have lost their ability to fly. Instead, they live in roosts on the ground. Like mammals, they use droppings to scent-mark their territory boundaries and will defend their home ranges aggressively from intruders, attacking unwelcome guests by lying on their backs and hitting out with their clawed feet.

In common with all birds, kiwis still have feathers and wings. However, their wings are so small that they are barely visible beneath the mass of long, hairlike feathers that cover their round bodies, like a fur coat. Bristly 'whiskers' around the bill are another useful, and very mammalian, addition to the kiwis' physique. These act as feelers to help them to find its way around as they feed in the dark. Their beaks, too, are more like an animal's snout, with nostrils at the tip for sniffing out food. Favourite meals are earthworms and insect larvae, but they will also eat seeds and berries.

'Eggs-hausting' Work

Most kiwis reach sexual maturity at two years of age and will begin looking for a mate during the late winter or early spring. In common with the cassowary, male kiwis are extremely active and attentive fathers. It is the male who builds the nest (this is usually in a hollow in the roots of a tree) and incubates the eggs once they have been laid. Kiwi eggs are huge compared to the mother's size,

Comparisons

Although very similar in appearance, the common brown kiwi (*Apteryx australis*) is the largest of the known species, weighing in at around 3.5kg (7.7lb). The little spotted (*Apteryx owenii*) is the smallest, at just 1kg (2.2lb). Specific species can also be distinguished by their plumages. Brown kiwis tend to be reddish brown in colour, while the little spotted has light banding on its body. This banding is even more apparent in the greater spotted kiwi (*Apteryx haastii*).

Greater spotted kiwi

Little spotted kiwi

Brown kiwi

weighing around 20 per cent of the female's body weight. Usually two eggs are laid, with a month's gap between each egg. For the couple, these eggs represent a massive investment in time and resources.

Kiwis have the longest incubation period of any bird – around 80 days. During this time, the male may lose up to one-fifth of its entire body weight, as it is unable to leave the nest to feed itself. Once hatched, though, the chicks will be independent and ready to start their own lives within a few weeks. A successful mating pair will usually stay together for life (up to 30 years) and breed every year.

Threats and Conservation

New Zealand has spent 80 million years isolated from the rest of the planet. This has allowed the island's wildlife to develop in ways that make it unique. Indeed, 80 per cent of New Zealand's trees, 25 per cent of its birds, 60 frogs and two bats are endemic to the island – this means that they are found nowhere else on Earth.

People arrived in New Zealand only 1000 years ago, yet it is from that time that species began to vanish. The first settlers, the Maoris, are believed to have hunted 11 species of moa bird to extinction. Later came the Europeans, who not only continued to hunt, but also introduced dogs, rats and stoats, against which native species had no defences at all – especially the birds that cannot fly. Fortunately, concerted action is now being taken to establish protected island sanctuaries, which are free of predators. This is to try to prevent species declining in numbers and eventually becoming extinct.

The male kiwi's powerful feet make quick work of the job of excavating a nest among the roots of a tree.

The female lays a huge egg. This is ten times the size of a chicken egg, although the female kiwi is barely bigger than a domestic hen.

The chick kicks its way out of its egg using its powerful feet. It emerges, with all its feathers and its eyes open.

Both parents feed the chick until it is old enough to fend for itself, which is at around two weeks old.

Malleefowl

The malleefowl is a shy and solitary bird, famed for building massive nest mounds to incubate its eggs. The population of this Australian 'bush turkey' has fallen by 30 per cent in just three generations, and the bird is now considered likely to become extinct.

Bill

Unlike the kiwi, the malleefowl has a short bill, which is not designed for specific food-gathering tasks. Instead, it is believed to contain heat-sensitive areas, which help the bird to judge the temperature of its nesting mound.

Key Facts	ORDER *Galliformes* / FAMILY *Megapodiidae* / GENUS & SPECIES *Leipoa ocellata*
Weight	Male 2–2.5kg (4.4–5.5lb); female 1.5–2kg (3.3–4.4lb)
Length	60cm (23.6in)
Wingspan	30–34cm (11.8–13.4in)
Sexual maturity	Usually 4 years
Breeding season	June–February, annually variable
Number of eggs	15 to 24
Incubation period	49–96 days, 62–64 days average
Fledging period	Independent on hatching
Breeding interval	Annual, but not during droughts or rainy periods
Typical diet	Omnivorous, but mainly eats buds, flowers, fruits, seeds
Life span	Up to 25 years

Tail
The short and stubby tail enables the malleefowl to manoeuvre swiftly through tangled undergrowth.

Feet
The malleefowl's large, clawed feet and powerful legs are the ideal design for digging soil. And that's just as well because a male may have to move 3 tonnes (3.3 tons) of dirt as it builds its nest mound, continually adjusting the temperature by adding and removing soil.

Mallefowl habitats

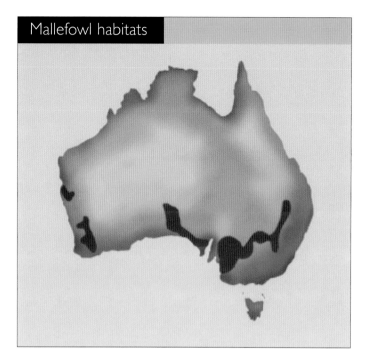

Malleefowl belong to a family of 22 species known as megapods, which means 'big feet'. Most megapods favour habitats with high rainfall and tropical climates, but malleefowl are not usual. As their name suggests, they live in semi-arid regions of South Australia, where mallee and eucalypts are the dominant vegetation.

Can't Fly, Won't Fly

Malleefowl are classed as a ground-dwelling bird, but this does not mean that they are flightless. Many Australasian species of bird, such as the emu, cassowary and kiwi, have lost the ability to fly.

Even if they had the inclination, their feathers are no longer rigid, and they lack the strong sternum that acts as an anchor for the bird's powerful flight muscles. Malleefowls can, and do, fly, but they seldom bother. Pairs of birds share a territory, and feed, build and tend their huge nest mounds on the ground. If they are disturbed by predators, they will usually freeze, presumably in the hope that, if they do not move, their patterned plumage will act as a natural protective camouflage. They will take to the air only if they are startled, in serious danger, or roosting overnight in the tree tops.

Construction Experts

Malleefowls incubate their eggs in huge nest mounds 1m (3ft 3in) high. Built from a mixture of soil and rotting vegetation, and similar to those which are constructed by alligators, these vast structures can take up to 11 months to build and maintain.

By constantly adding and removing soil and using their bills as thermometers, malleefowl are able to keep these mounds at between 32° and 34°C (90° and 93°F). This is

Comparisons

Malleefowls are closely related to the ground-dwelling maleos (*Macrocephalon maleo*) of Sulawesi. Maleos can be easily identified by their distinctive black-and-white plumage and a characteristic casque on the top of their head.

Maleo

Malleefowl

perfect for incubating eggs. Malleefowl mate for life and the breeding pair will lay up to 30 eggs in a season. As each egg weighs 10 per cent of the female's body weight, this is a huge strain for such a small bird, so egg-laying is spaced out – usually one egg every three to seven days. While the male tends the mound, the female spends much of her time foraging for food to keep her up her strength.

Once the eggs have hatched, the chicks must fight their way out of the mound, using their feet to dig to the surface. This exhausting process can take 15 hours. Once free, they will then roll to the bottom of the mound and scurry into the bush – completely unaided by their parents. If they survive (and only 2 per cent do), they will be able to fly by within 24 hours.

Threats and Conservation

Destruction of habitat has had a massive effect on the numbers of malleefowl. It is estimated that around 36 per cent of traditional mallee forests have been removed to make way for plantations and commercial farming, but by far the greatest threat to malleefowl habitat is from bushfires. Indigenous people have set fires for centuries to assist in hunting and land management. When Europeans arrived, they changed the fire regimes, removing many fire corridors. The result has been huge bushfires, which can devastate entire regions. A national plan is now in place to address this and the many other problems faced by the malleefowl, but the future remains uncertain for this stocky little ground dweller.

Malleefowl eggs can take 50–100 days to incubate. The exact time depends on the temperature in the mound, which the birds check using their beaks.

If the mound gets too hot, the malleefowl simply scrapes away the excess soil and rotting vegetation, which allows it to cool down.

If it is too cold, more material is added to the mound. The majority of this work is done by the male.

Emerging from the mound, the chick is blind and alone. It must survive entirely on its own, as it gets no help from its parents.

Numbat

With its rusty-coloured fur, banded back and bristly tail, the numbat is impossible to mistake for anything else. This rare small marsupial has the distinction of being Western Australia's mammal emblem — a status that may well save this unique species from extinction.

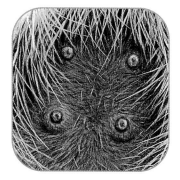

Mammae

Numbat young are not able to shelter in their mother's pouch for protection. Instead, they simply cling onto her teats, protected by a mass of thick hair.

Key Facts	ORDER *Dasyuromorphia* / FAMILY *Myrmecobiidae* GENUS & SPECIES *Myrmecobius fasciatus*	
Weight	Male 350–700g (12–25oz); female 275–550g (10–19oz)	
Length Head & Body Tail	23–27cm (9–10.6in) 17–21cm (6.7–8.3in)	
Shoulder height	12–15cm (4.7–5.9in)	
Sexual maturity	Male 2 years; female 1 year	
Mating season	January	
Gestation period	14 days	
Number of young	Exact number unknown, but only up to four can survive because the female has only four mammae	
Birth interval	1 year	
Typical diet	Mainly termites	
Life span	3–5 years	

Feet
The numbat's front feet have five toes; its hind feet have four. Each are designed as digging tools, with long toes and curved claws to enable the numbat to plough through the earth with ease.

Coat
The coats of numbats are coloured grey-brown to red-brown, with horizontal white stripes across its back and rump. Six to ten stripes are usual, but the exact number and spacing are unique to each individual, like fingerprints.

This specialized and unique marsupial is the only member of the family Myrmecobiidae, and one of Western Australia's most famous and distinctive, wild inhabitants.

Early Models

Modern mammals are placental: the unborn young grow inside their mother's body, where they are supplied with nutrients and oxygen by an organ called a 'placenta'. It is only once the young are fully formed that they are born. Marsupials are an early model of mammal, with a much more basic design. Their young are born at an extremely immature stage of development: tiny, blind and almost limbless. To survive, they must crawl through their mother's fur until they reach a pouch called the 'marsupium', which is where the name 'marsupial' comes from. Here they attach themselves to a teat, which provides enough nutrients, in the form of milk, for them to finish their development.

The numbat is unusual in that it is a marsupial, but does not have a pouch. Instead, the babies are protected from the elements by a thick layer of hair surrounding the teats. After birth, which usually takes place between January and May, the young will make their way to the teats and stay attached there, feeding, for around three months. They will then be deposited in a protective burrow until they are weaned, which may take a further two months.

Snack Attack

The lack of a pouch is not the only unique feature of the numbat. Most marsupials are nocturnal and feed under cover of night. Numbats are diurnal: they are active during

Numbat habitats

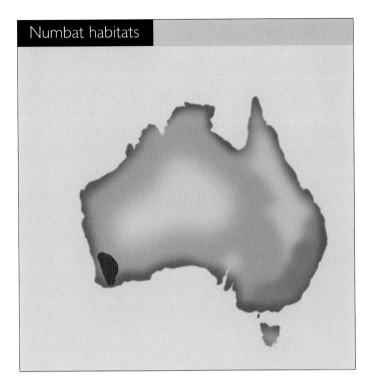

the day, when they spend much of their time foraging for food. In nature, animals who are successful tend to exploit a specific habitat or food resource, and the numbat has cornered the market on insects. In fact, it is the only marsupial to feed on insects – in particular, the termites that inhabit fallen logs or leaf litter in eucalyptus forests.

To track a potential meal, numbats walk with their nose to the ground, sniffing out the termites by scent. They then dig them up with their powerful claws, and lick up any escapees with their long, sticky tongue. A hungry

Comparisons

In common with numbats, quolls live mainly in forested areas and often use hollowed-out logs as a den. Like many hunters, quolls are nocturnal. Known as tiger cats, these fierce little marsupials are much more predatory than their numbat relatives, and will make a meal of almost anything. However, habitat loss and competition from introduced species have made them increasingly rare.

Numbat

Quoll

numbat can consume around 20,000 termites a day. That's a sizeable snack, comprising around 10 per cent of their entire body weight. They do not specifically eat ants, but their preference has earned them their other common name: the banded anteater.

Threats and Conservation

In the past, the Earth's land formed one huge, united mass called Pangaea. This 'super continent' began to move apart around 200 million years ago. One half formed Laurasia, which eventually split again to create Europe, North America and Asia. The other half, Gondwanaland, ultimately became Africa, Antarctica, Australia and South America. It was during this schism that Australasia became isolated from the rest of the world, preserving its unique flora and fauna until the arrival of European settlers in 1788. With them came new predatory species such as the fox and the domestic cat, and new ways of living, which destroyed many of the numbat's traditional habitats.

This combination of factors brought the numbat to the brink of extinction just a few years ago. Now, numbers of this marsupial are stabilizing, thanks to coordinated and well-orchestrated conservation efforts. Fox control programmes, for example, have allowed existing numbat populations to begin to recover, while captive-bred individuals have been reintroduced into fox-free areas. The numbat is still listed as 'Vulnerable', but populations look secure for the present.

During the night, a numbat shelters in a hollowed-out log, which is too narrow for predators to enter.

As day breaks, the numbat ventures out into the forest in search of a tasty termite snack.

Detecting a termite colony, the numbat digs away at the soil to expose the termite galleries below.

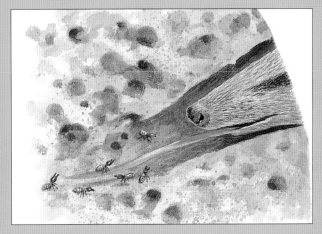

Its sticky tongue is 10cm (4in) long, and the numbat uses it to lap up any escaping termites.

Potoroo

Potoroos are also known as rat kangaroos because that is exactly what they look like. Growing to rabbit size, potoroos share many of the characteristics of their larger kangaroo cousins. With long feet and a tail for balance, these mini marsupials are one of Australia's rarest species.

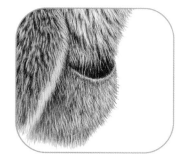

Pouch

Most marsupials carry their immature young in a pouch called a marsupium. Inside, the tiny, blind and almost limbless babies attach themselves to a teat and begin to feed. Long-footed potoroos remain in the pouch for 140–150 days before they are ready to become independent.

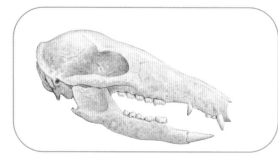

Skull

This potoroo's skull displays all the features we would expect from an animal with an elongated snout, long face and small head.

Key Facts	ORDER *Diprotodontia* / FAMILY *Potoroidae* GENUS & SPECIES *Potorous longipes, P. tridactylus*	
Weight	Male 740–2200g (26–78oz); female 660–1800g (23–63oz)	
Length Head and body Tail	15–100mm (¹/2–4in) 20–33cm (7.8–12.9in)	
Sexual maturity	1 year	
Mating season	Year round	
Gestation period	38 days	
Number of young	1	
Birth interval	4–6 months	
Typical diet	Fungi, insects, grass and roots	
Life span	At least 7 years in the wild; 12 years in captivity	

Potoroo habitats

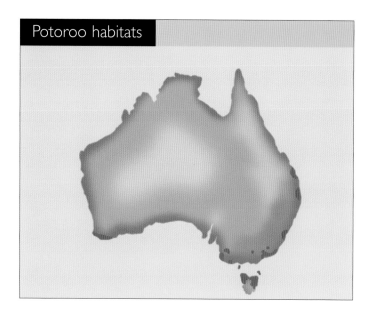

There are three known species of potoroo: the long-footed (*Potorous longipes*), the long-nosed potoroo (*Potorous tridactylus*) and Gilbert's potoroo (*Potorous gilbertii*). Of these, Gilbert's is the rarest, and was believed to be extinct until its rediscovery in 1994.

Back from the Dead

The first, and until recently, the only documented sighting of Gilbert's potoroo was by the English naturalist John

Gilbert (1812–1845), in 1840. In his account, he described 'a little animal' that inhabited 'dense thickets of spearwood and rank vegetation around swamps or small running streams'. He also recorded how local aboriginals hunted the potoroo for food: '… the natives capture it by treading down sticks and forming a long narrow passage through the thicket, and by beating the bush and making a yelling noise, drive the affrighted animals before them …'

It was generally assumed that such hunting parties had wiped out this little marsupial until Elizabeth Sinclair, a student, discovered a small surviving colony, right where Gilbert had originally found them – in Two People's Bay Reserve near King George Sound in Western Australia.

You Scratch My Back …

Potoroos are reclusive by nature, spending much of their day in a small nest, hollowed out beneath forest vegetation. They come out at night to forage, but are still rarely seen, as they usually burrow beneath the leaf litter, leaving only a telltale trail of debris behind them. This adaptable marsupial will eat anything from insect larvae to fruit, but feeds mainly on fungi.

The long-footed potoroo can be found in a variety of forest types at150–1000m (490–3280ft) above sea level. Long-nosed potoroos are more widespread, occurring on both coastal heath land and rainforest. But what these

Comparisons

As these illustrations show, bettongs and potoroos are very similar in appearance, although potoroos tend to be slightly larger in size on average. They also share similar diets. This means that they are often found in the same type of habitats, and so have suffered a similar decline in numbers.

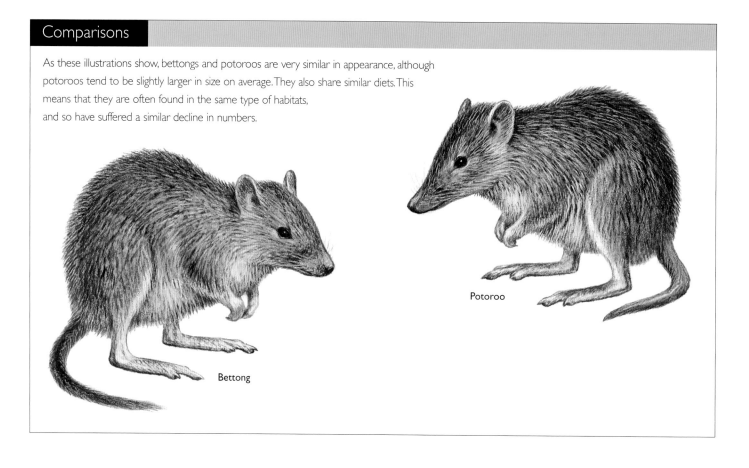

Bettong

Potoroo

habitats have in common is that they are damp, which is exactly the conditions fungus need to grow. In these environments, the potoroos form a vital part of the web of life. The fungus needs damp conditions, such as those beneath leaf litter, to flourish. So it provides the trees with nutrients and helps them to resist disease. The potoroo relies on the forest for shelter and the fungus for food. When it eats the fungus, the spores pass through its body and out as waste. So, the more fungus it eats, the more spores it spreads, inadvertently protecting the forest and seeding it with more food along the way.

Threats and Conservation

Usually, in any environment, animals compete with each other to take best advantage of the local habitat and food.

The most successful animals become the dominant species while others, less successful, may die out. Until the arrival of settlers, Australasia's strange and wonderful animals had been safe in their established niches for 200 million years. Then, suddenly, came the arrival of bigger, faster and more aggressive species.

Foxes, dogs, cats, rats and rabbits were all introduced to Australia and had a devastating effect on the native wildlife. Foxes, dogs and cats predate them, while rabbits and rats compete with them for food. There is no immediate solution to this problem, but in recent years attempts have been made to control introduced species, with limited success. Special management areas have also been established which, it is hoped, will benefit not just potoroos, but also other endangered species such as quolls.

A potoroo bounds across the forest floor, jumping on its hind legs like a full-sized kangaroo.

Digging around in the damp soil, the potoroo forages for its favourite food – fungus.

A mushroom makes a big feast for an animal that grows no bigger than a rabbit.

The potoroo is an opportunist and will gladly add small insects to its diet.

ARCTIC OCEAN

Brooks Range

Mackenzie Mts

ALASKA

CANADA

Rocky Mountains

Hudson
Bay

LABRADOR
SEA

NORTH
PACIFIC
OCEAN

Sierra Nevada

UNITED
STATES

Appalachian Mts

NORTH
ATLANTIC
OCEAN

Gulf of
Mexico

North America

North America is the world's third biggest continent in area, but is unarguably the largest in scale. This region of rugged natural beauty includes snow-dusted peaks, towering waterfalls, sun-blasted canyons, sweeping grasslands and a truly dazzling array of wildlife.

For 15,000 years, North America's earliest inhabitants lived in relative harmony with their environment, revering the animals that provided them with food. Europeans began to arrive on this vast and diverse continent around 600 years ago, but their impact has been much more dramatic: the region is home to around 8 per cent of the world's entire population, but there are now few parts of it that are as wild and untamed as the land found by the early settlers.

In just a few centuries, land where unique species once thrived has been converted into farms, cities and factories. In some regions, undesirable species such as rattlesnakes have even been driven to the brink of extinction by settlers seeking to make their new home safe. The greatest loss of all has been the Great Plains. These enormous grasslands once formed the heart of this great continent. Today, in the 'Prairie State' of Illinois, just 1416.4 hectares (3500 acres) out of 13.9 million hectares (37 million acres) remain of this vital wildlife habitat.

In 2004, 73 Canadian and some 903 native US species were listed by the IUCN as 'Critically Endangered', 'Endangered' or 'Vulnerable'. However, there is hope. Conservation groups – both public and private – are now working hard to preserve the remaining wild spaces.

Black-footed Ferret

In 1987, after decades during which their numbers declined rapidly, North America's black-footed ferret finally became officially 'Extinct in the Wild'. Thanks to a lot of hard work and perseverance, however, this was not the end of the story for this bright-eyed little mustalid.

Scent glands

In common with weasels, skunks and wolverines, ferrets mark their territory using a potent and very smelly liquid which they discharge from scent glands, hidden under the tail.

Key Facts	ORDER *Carnivora* / FAMILY *Mustelidae* GENUS & SPECIES *Mustela nigripes*
Weight	0.9–1.4kg (2–3lb)
Head and body	38–60cm (15–24in)
Tail	12–15cm (5–6in)
Sexual maturity	1 year
Breeding season	March and April
Gestation period	6 weeks
Number of young	1–6
Typical diet	Prairie dogs and other small mammals
Life span	3–4 years in the wild; 8–9 in captivity

Eyes
Large forward-facing eyes tell us that this animal is a hunter, as 'binocular' vision helps predators to judge distances more accurately.

Legs
Ferrets, along with other members of the Mustelidae family, have very short legs. This helps them to travel with ease through narrow underground tunnels in pursuit of their prey.

Comparisons

With their long, low-slung bodies, small heads and thick fur, black-footed ferrets seem like typical members of *Mustelidae* family. Yet wolverines also belong to the same group of mammals and are much stockier than their slim-bodied relatives. They also have a particularly heavy, bear-like head. This large head contains powerful jaws which enable the wolverine to crunch through most meals, even frozen carrion.

Black-footed ferret   Wolverine

It is a sad fact that, as the world becomes more industrialized and populations grow, an increasing number of animals will vanish for ever. In the 1980s, it looked like the black-footed ferret would become yet another casualty of this trend.

The Beginning of the End

For this alert and agile mammal, home was the grasslands of North America's Great Plains. Here, the ferret lived on a diet made up almost exclusively of prairie dogs. In fact, in a year a typical family of four would munch their way through 700 a year.

During the mid 1900s a programme began to eradicate the prairie dog, which was considered a pest to farming. The effect on the black-footed ferret was devastating. Indeed, the effects were felt by more than just ferrets. Populations of many other species – burrowing owls, mountain plovers and golden eagles – who also relied on the prairie dog for food, fell rapidly, too. The removal of one 'pest' meant that the whole ecosystem of the Great Plains began to disintegrate. Suddenly, the black-footed ferret was one of the world's most endangered mammals.

More Bad News

The main reason for ridding the plains of the prairie dogs was to help farmers, and by the 1990s the enormous grasslands which once formed the heart of the great

North American landmass had almost disappeared. In just 150 years, 99 per cent of the region's wild grasslands had been converted into farmland. The ferrets, along with many other species, seemed doomed. In 1985, however,

Black-footed ferret habitats

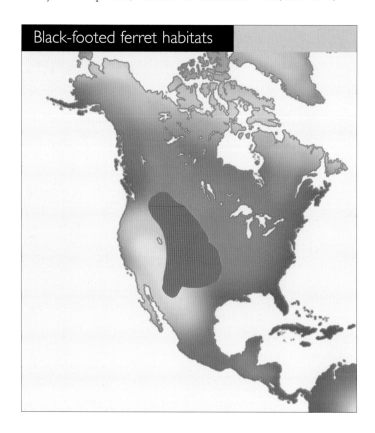

the Wyoming Game and Fish Department decided to act. Working with the US Fish & Wildlife Service, it captured six black-footed ferrets from one of Wyoming's last known wild ferret populations. The aim was to initiate a captive breeding programme before it was too late. Unfortunately it was discovered that two of the six ferrets they captured were infected with dog distemper and, before they could be isolated, all of them died. With the situation now urgent, it was decided to capture the last known wild ferrets and vaccinate them. The plan worked, and by 1986 there were 18 healthy ferrets in captivity.

Threats and Conservation

What happened next is a story which should warm the hearts of conservationists everywhere. After a very shaky start, the captive breeding programme was soon producing healthy baby ferrets ('kits') every year. In 1988, the Black-footed Ferret Recovery Plan was published and declared its aim of maintaining a constant captive breeding population of 240 ferrets. These would be divided into a number of separate populations, to ensure that the whole population could not be wiped out by disease – as had so nearly happened in 1985. A ferret sperm bank was even established to ensure that, should disaster strike, there would still be some hope.

Populations of black-footed ferrets have now been reintroduced into the states of Arizona, Colorado, South Dakota, Montana, Utah and Wyoming. For once, the future of a species which was threatened with extinction looks truly hopeful.

Black-footed ferrets choose to live in abandoned burrows which used to belong to their favourite prey – the prairie dog.

Life on the plains can be dangerous.! Fortunately, ferrets have not only excellent eyesight, but also hearing.

Ever alert for danger, the ferret cautiously creeps out of its borrowed burrow, taking care to check for predators.

Desert Tortoise

The great tragedy of the desert tortoise is that this ancient and successful species – which lived through the first Ice Age – should be unable to survive in the modern world.

Key Facts	ORDER *Chelonia*
	FAMILY *Testudinidae*
	GENUS & SPECIES *Gopherus agassizii*

Weight	11–23kg (24–51lb)
Length	Up to 37cm (14.5in)
Sexual maturity	14–20 years
Breeding season	Early summer
Number of eggs	2–14
Hatching period	About 100 days
Breeding interval	1–3 clutches a year
Typical diet	Grasses, herbs, cacti
Life span	Up to 100 years

Shell

The tortoise's upper shell (or carapace) and the yellowish, lower shell (or plastron) are both made from keratin, which is the same material as nails and horses' hooves. Yet they also contain nerves and a blood supply, which means that any damage to the inner part of the shell is extremely painful.

Feet

Wide, powerful feet, tipped with long claws, enable the desert tortoise to walk and burrow through the earth with ease.

Mouth

The desert tortoise has a pair of horny jaws, which resemble a bird's bill. The edges are serrated, which enables the tortoise to cut up tough vegetation.

Comparisons

Desert tortoises are almost entirely vegetarian. Their aquatic cousins Sonoran mud turtles (*Kinosternon sonoriense sonoriense*) spend their

lives in shallow mud pools and rivers, where they feed on insects and crustaceans. As much of their lives are spent in water, they also have webbed feet and a more streamlined carapace.

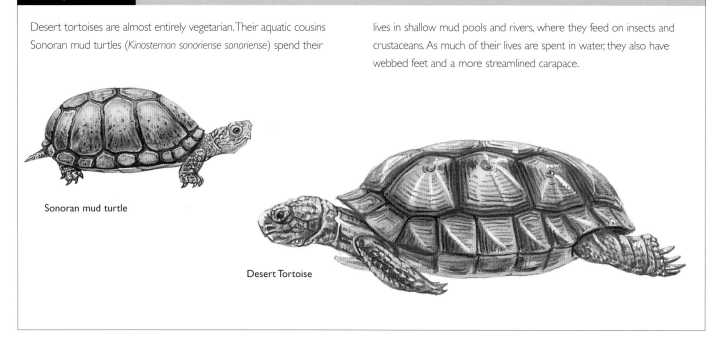

Sonoran mud turtle

Desert Tortoise

Wild tortoises can be found throughout the world, except in Australia and Polynesia. Desert tortoises are one of the few species of the genus *Gosperus*, which are native to North America.

Built to Last

Desert tortoises have changed little in 30 million years. Why should they? They have a winning formula. These tough desert inhabitants are ideally adapted for a life in

Desert tortoise habitats

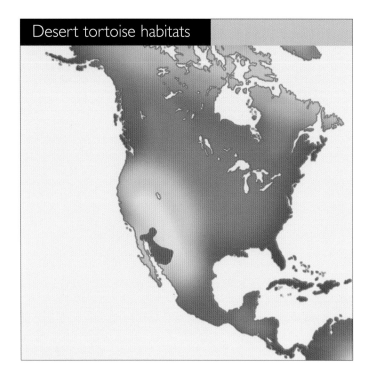

some of North America's most arid regions. Tortoises are cold-blooded reptiles. Their blood is the same temperature as their surroundings so, to stay alive, they must keep warm and avoid extreme cold. For this reason, they are most active during the early morning and evening, when they spend their time grazing on vegetation. During the coldest winter months, they hibernate in deep burrows, which they either dig themselves (in the case of Mohave Desert tortoises) or adapt from existing mammals burrows (as is more common for Sonoran Desert tortoises). They are also dormant during the hottest part of the summer – a behaviour called 'aestivation'.

Desert tortoises also have an incredible ability to conserve liquid. Most of the liquid in their diet comes from vegetation, but they will drink copious amounts of water when it is available. A large bladder enables them to hold 40 per cent of their body weight in water and uric acid. Over time, the wastes are ejected, while the vital water is reabsorbed.

Shell Suits

The term 'tortoise' is almost always used when we talk about terrestrial species. Turtles are generally aquatic. What most of the 270 known species of turtles and tortoise have in common is their shell. In tortoises, these distinctive, high domes are made up of light to dark brown plates called 'scutes', which are fused to the axial skeleton – the bones that comprise the skull and backbone. The upper part of the shell, called the 'carapace', has around 38 scutes. The lower, called the 'plastron', has 12 to 14.

As tortoises cannot shed their skin like snakes, the tough carapace and plastron must grow with them. Generally, additional scutes are not added to the shell; instead, existing scutes grow in size. We can see this by the radiating lines of yellow and black on the carapace, which are growth lines. Despite popular belief, tortoises do not actually live in their shells. Their homes are in burrows in the ground or beneath vegetation. But their shells do make very effective temporary shelters, as tortoises are able to withdraw their feet and head into it for protection when in danger.

Threats and Conservation
In many parts of the world, deserts are the last great wildernesses, where nature flourishes simply because the environment is too extreme and too harsh for humans to tolerate. In developed countries such as the United States, however, technology is making these areas increasingly accessible. And as the miners and settlers move in, the existing wildlife suffers.

In the case of the desert tortoise, the problem is not just habitat loss. These are slow-moving creatures, and hundreds are killed every year by recreational vehicles. They are also popular in the pet trade, although wild tortoises rarely survive long in captivity. Listed as 'Threatened' by the US Endangered Species Act, and 'Vulnerable' by the IUCN, these long-lived reptiles are now legally protected, and attempts are being made to set aside protected regions for tortoise conservation.

Desert tortoises hatch in the summer, around four months after eggs have been laid. The temperature in the nest determines the sex of the hatchlings.

It can take five years for the juvenile tortoise's shell to harden. During this time, they are extremely vulnerable to predators and the mortality rate is very high.

Reaching sexual maturity at around 15 years of age, desert tortoises will begin to look for mates with which to breed in early May.

After mating, the males return to their burrows. The females will lay up to five eggs, which are buried in the sand and left to hatch unattended.

Greater Prairie Chicken

This popular and attractive native of the American Midwest was once a common sight, but numbers have declined so dramatically in the past two decades that this stocky brown bird is listed as 'Vulnerable' by the IUCN.

Female
Male and female greater prairie chickens are a similar size and coloration, but females lack the distinctive yellow-orange air sac beneath the eyes. They also have shorter pinnae and barred tail feathers.

Male

Stiff, winglike feathers (pinnae) around the neck identify this prairie chicken as a male. He also has an enlarged yellow-orange air sac beneath his eye. These are pink-purple in the lesser greater prairie chicken (*Tympanuchus cupido pinnatus*).

Key Facts	ORDER *Galliformes* / FAMILY *Tetraonidae* GENUS & SPECIES *Tympanuchus cupido*
Weight	Male 900–1400g (2–3 lb); Female 450–900g (1–2 lb)
Length	41–48cm (16–19in)
Wingspan	56cm (22in)
Sexual maturity	1 year
Breeding season	March–May
Number of eggs	11 or 12
Incubation period	23–25 days
Fledging period	8–10 weeks
Breeding interval	1 year
Typical diet	Insects, buds, prairie grass, seeds, leaves and grains
Life span	2 years

Comparisons

The greatest difference between the greater prairie chicken and the sharp-tailed grouse (*Tympanuchus phasianellus*) is their tails. Both birds are comparable in size and shape, with a similar air sac beneath their eyes. The grouse, as its name suggests, is identifiable by its long pointed tail, which is often used in courtship displays. The prairie chicken's tail is shorter and more rounded.

Sharp-tailed grouse

Greater prairie chicken

Greater prairie chickens belong to a cosmopolitan family, Tetraonidae, which can be identified by their short wings, rounded tails and feathered feet. Members of this family include wild grouse, capercaillie and ptarmigans – species that are all currently declining in numbers.

Look at Me!
In common with kakapos, great prairie chickens have a 'lek' breeding system. During the mating season, male cocks will leave their traditional territories to establish

Greater prairie chicken habitats

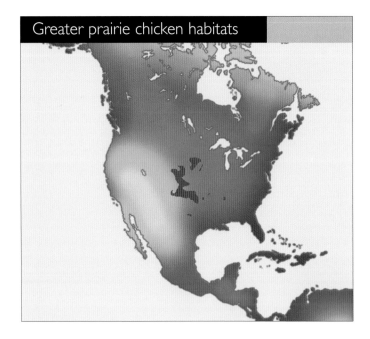

their own mating courts. Competition during this time is fierce, and each male will fight to secure the best sites in the lek, or arena. Once established, males begin a series of elaborate displays and calls designed to attract a mate. These displays are particularly impressive at dawn, when males can be heard making loud booming calls, stamping their feet, leaping and posturing.

During this period, the male's orange–yellow air sac, which is called a tympani, becomes inflated, and their long pinnae neck feathers stand on end, like a pair of horns. This all adds up to a magnificent display, which the male hopes will secure him the right to mate with one of the females. If mating is successful, the female will lay ten to twelve eggs. Greater prairie chickens usually mate only once a year; however, if the nest is disturbed or destroyed, a female may breed twice in the same season.

Home on the Range
Prairie chickens roost on the ground, using thick vegetation to give them shelter and hide them from predators. In the winter, when vegetation is sparse, they burrow beneath the snow. Digging around 25cm (10in) down, these industrious birds create horizontal roosting chambers, which use the insulating properties of the snow to keep them warm – the same principle that makes igloos such effective shelters.

Prairie chickens are gregarious birds and form winter flocks of up to 300 individuals. With food scarce during these harsh months, such huge numbers provides them with additional security from predators. As their name implies, greater prairie chickens are most at home on the rolling plains of the Midwest. These regions used to provide the chicken with the perfect habitat – a mix of long and short grasses, wetlands (known as prairie potholes) and thick scrub. Much of this land is now used to grow grain, which has been added to the chicken's traditional diet of leaves, seeds, insects and berries.

Threats and Conservation

Of the greater prairie chicken's three known subspecies, the heath hen (*Tympanuchus cupido cupido*) is already extinct, Attwater's prairie chicken (*Tympanuchus cupido attwateri*) is endangered, and the greater prairie chicken (*Tympanuchus cupido pinnatus*) is vulnerable. Surprisingly,

the greater prairie chicken is still numerous enough in four US states to be legally hunted, yet it is considered endangered in at least 15 other states. Such discrepancies serve to highlight just how dramatically habitat loss can affect local wildlife.

The Great Plains were once one of the world's great grassland habitats, covering a quarter of North America, from Mexico to Southern Canada. The 1960 Homestead Act, which opened the way for people to settle the prairies, was the beginning of the conversion of the plains to farms. In many cases, prairie chickens have adapted to this new agricultural environment, but they still need thick vegetation for nesting. Their future lies in working with local communities to control overgrazing and lay aside land where these native birds can flourish.

Male Greater Prairie Chickens gather together at special 'lekking sites' in the spring, at the start of the mating season.

The males fight to establish their dominance and the right to occupy ground in the centre of the 'booming arena'.

Competition to mate is fierce and males strut, leap, stomp and emit sonorous booms to attract a female.

The aim of such acrobatics is to prove to the female that he is fit enough to sire her young.

North American Lungless Salamanders

Often spending their lives under vegetation, in streams and cave systems, the salamanders of North America are a rare sight in the wild. Increasingly threatened by water depletion and pollution, these secretive amphibians may soon be extinct.

Gills

Many salamanders begin life as aquatic larva. To enable them to breathe under water, they have gills, which are lost as they grow to adulthood.

Mouth

The salamander's mouth contains two scent lobes, or nares. When hunting for food, this unique amphibian uses these lobes to taste the air for its prey's scent.

Eyes

Most species of salamander have huge, forward-pointing eyes, which enable them to accurately judge distances when hunting. The special scent lobes in their mouths are so sensitive, however, that some cave-dwelling species are totally blind.

Key Facts	ORDER *Urodela* / FAMILY *Plethodontidae* / GENUS & SPECIES Various
Weight	Varies from a few grams up to 30g (1oz)
Length	5–22cm (2–8.6in)
Sexual maturity	Up to 5 years
Breeding season	Summer to late winter; varies between species
Number of eggs	10–100
Hatching period	1.5–12 months
Larval stage	1–36 months
Breeding interval	1 year
Typical diet	Larva feeds on small aquatic animals; adult feeds on snails, earthworms, insects and smaller species of salamander
Life span	Up to 25 years

There are up to 90 species of lungless salamander in North America, many of which are currently considered to be 'Vulnerable' or 'Endangered' by the IUCN.

Every Breath You Take

Salamanders may look like lizards, but they are amphibians not reptiles, which means that they are related to frogs and toads. Most amphibians are cold-blooded animals and spend part or all of their lives in water. Hatching from eggs laid in rivers, ponds or on damp vegetation, tiny larvae may spend from six weeks to five years in this juvenile form, depending on the species. As they reach adulthood, a remarkable metamorphosis takes place and the young salamanders lose their gills, develop lungs and legs, and begin to grow a tail – ready for a life on land. Some amphibians have both gills and lungs, but salamanders of the family Plenthodontidae are lungless. Instead, they take in air through their skin and the lining of the mouth. Breathing with gills means that oxygen is pushed into the body by movement through the water as the creature swims. The salamander's skin is semi-permeable, allowing gasses to pass straight through the thin membrane into the bloodstream. This is a primitive method, but the result is the same: to exchange oxygen and carbon dioxide between the blood cells and the outside world.

Damp Dens

Lungless salamanders cannot live in dry conditions. Their skin needs to be kept moist, or they suffocate. Despite this, they are found in a wide range of diverse habitats. Moisture

For some species, such as this common red salamander, mating takes place underwater, in the summer or early autumn.

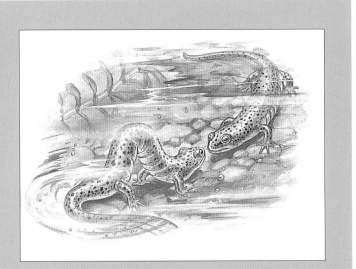

After an energetic display, the male deposits a small package of sperm, called a 'spermatophore', in front of the female.

The female gently picks up the package, using her hind legs to guide the parcel into her egg tube.

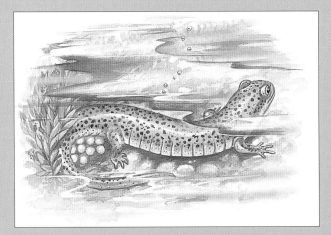

Weeks or even months later, hundreds of tiny eggs are laid. These are attached to stones or vegetation for safety.

is the common theme. Whether they live in ponds, swamps, caves or forests, they need a moist retreat to call home. Terrestrial salamanders are hard to spot because of this. They often burrow beneath mud, damp vegetation, stones or rotting logs, where they spend much of the day.

At night, salamanders come out to hunt. Using scent glands in their mouths, called 'nares', they suck in air and taste it for the telltale chemical signals that tell them that prey is near. Most adult salamanders are carnivores and dine on a varied menu, depending on their habitat and size. Many salamanders are just a few centimetres long, but some grow to 1.5m (4ft 11in) and can make a meal of fish, large amphibians and even other salamanders.

Threats and Conservation

Worldwide, there are around 536 known species of lungless salamanders, which belong to the family Plethodontidae. Some lungless species are also classified as members of the subfamily Desmognathinae. Many of these rare amphibians are found in only very specific habitats, which means that sudden changes can potentially wipe out an entire species. For example, the Texas blind salamander (*Eurycea rathbuni*) can be found only in the water-filled caverns of Edwards Aquifer, near San Marcos, Texas. The Blanco blind salamander (*Eurycea robusta*) occurs only in the Balcones Aquifer, near Blanco River, Texas. Both of these are on the US endangered species register. The Georgetown salamander (*Eurycea naufragia*) is so rare that it

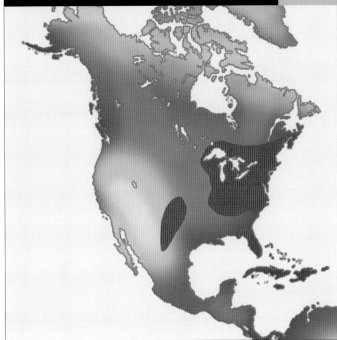

North American salamander habitats

has been seen only a few times since it was discovered in 1999. All of these unique amphibians are under serious threat from water depletion and pollution, as the cities around them grow. There is no simple solution, but unless a way can be found to accommodate the needs of the local people and the wildlife, they may soon vanish for ever.

Comparisons

Most of North America's salamanders grow to a length of no more than 22cm (8.6in), yet they have a gargantuan relative: the giant Japanese salamander (*Andrias japonicus*). This huge amphibian lives its entire life in the water, but breathes through its skin, just like other lungless salamanders.

Red salamander

Japanese giant salamander

West Indian Manatee

Manatees are the stuff of legend: the reality behind the old sailors' stories about mermaids. Once widespread along the Gulf of Mexico and the West Indies, these passive and shy mammals are one of the United States' great wild treasures.

Head and snout

At the tip of the manatee's bulbous head is a blunt snout and a pair of mobile, bristle-covered lips, which are used to pluck up bunches of aquatic vegetation.

Key Facts

ORDER *Sirenidae* / **FAMILY** *Trichechidae* / **GENUS & SPECIES** *Trichechus manatus*

Weight	200–500kg (440–1102lb)
Length	2.5–4.5m (8ft 3in–14ft 9in)
Sexual maturity	6–10 years
Mating season	No set mating season
Gestation period	Approximately 12 months
Number of young	1
Birth interval	2–5 years
Typical diet	Vegetation, especially sea grasses
Life span	Up to 30 years in captivity, probably longer in the wild

Teeth

Unlike most mammals, the
West Indian manatee has molar
teeth that grow constantly.
As the teeth at the front of the
manatee's mouth are worn
down, new teeth at the back
of the jaw move forward to
replace them.

Flippers

The manatee's flippers are
more like hands, rather than
traditional flippers – and they
are used in much the same way.
In fact, they are just as useful
for digging up and holding
vegetation as for swimming.

There are two known families of sea cows: the Caribbean and Atlantic manatees (Trichechidae) and the dugongs (Dugongidae) of the Indian Ocean. Steller's sea cow (*Hydrodamalis stelleri*) once ranged throughout the North Pacific, but became extinct in 1768.

Sea Cows

In the distant past, the ancestors of today's land dwellers lived in the oceans. The move from sea to land took many millennia, but it probably began simply enough. A group of fish began to hunt closer to the shore, where the pickings were easier. Over time, the fish that were better able to tolerate the shallows became more successful. They had more food, so they produced more offspring, and these in turn inherited the same survival traits from their parents. What is surprising is that, having conquered the land, some animals – such as the manatee – decided to return to the water.

Manatees belong to the order Sirenidae, which are commonly called Sea Cows. Sirenians are members of a group called Tethytheria which also encompass elephants and hyraxes and are the manatee's closest land relatives.

Shallow Breathing

Manatees spend their lives in shallow coastal waters, estuaries, bays and canals, usually no more than 1.8m (6ft) deep. They are only partially adapted to an aquatic life and still have hair on their bodies and nails on their flippers. The biggest clue to the Manatee's land-bound past, though is that these sedate, aquatic mammals must come to the

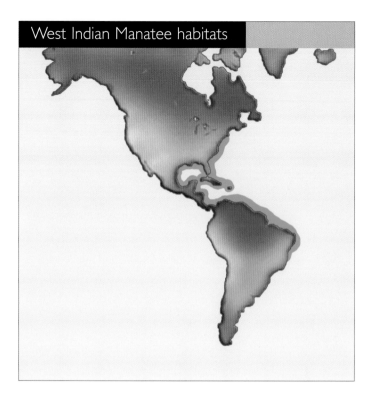

West Indian Manatee habitats

surface of the water to breathe. Manatees are completely vegetarian, and spend much of their day grazing on aquatic plants and resting in the warm shallows. When using such a small amount of energy, they surface for air every five to 20 minutes. Manatees are generally slow-moving, rarely swimming faster than 7km/h (4.3mph), but when in danger they are capable of reaching up to 25km/h (15.5mph). During such athletic displays, they

Comparisons

Manatees and dugongs (*Dugong dugong*) belong to the same animal order. It is not surprising, then, that they share many similarities. Both are herbivores and live primarily in warm coastal waters. Unlike manatees, dugongs are much better adapted for an aquatic life. They have lost their body hair and nails, and have a more fishlike tail, to propel them through the water.

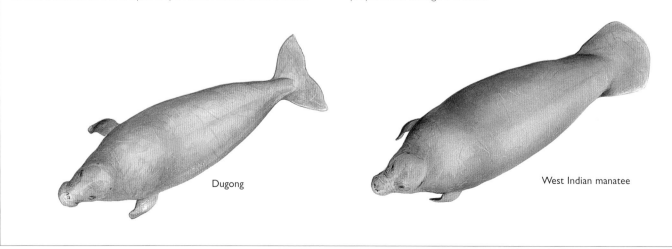

Dugong

West Indian manatee

need to surface to breathe every 30 seconds – like a sprinter gulping for air.

Threats and Conservation

Manatees have no natural enemies so it seems peculiar to think that the number of these mammals is dramatically declining, it is due to humans that this particular animal is at risk of dying out. Manatees used to be extensively hunted for their meat and blubber, which was rendered down to make oil. Today, they are legally protected throughout the United States under the Marine Mammal Protection Act of 1972, the Endangered Species Act of 1973 and the Florida Manatee Sanctuary Act, 1978. Under these laws, anyone found intentionally or negligently harming or harassing a manatee faces up to a year in jail and a $100,000 fine. Yet every year around 100 manatees are killed.

The culprits are not people but boats. The manatee's habit of basking in the shallows makes them vulnerable to high-speed pleasure crafts. They also get trapped in crab lines, on fishing hooks and drowned in canal locks. In Florida's Upper St John's River and the north-west region, the solution has been to make the entire area into a protected zone, with speed restrictions on all boats entering the waters. It has taken 30 years, but manatee populations within these protected zones are starting to increase. This small population represents only 16 per cent of the entire US manatee population – which currently numbers 3000. The task now facing local administrations is how to replicate Florida's success nationwide.

Manatees breed all year round, but an average pair will give birth to just one calf every two to five years.

A year after mating, a manatee calf is born, tail first. This bouncing baby may be up to 1m (3ft 3in) in length.

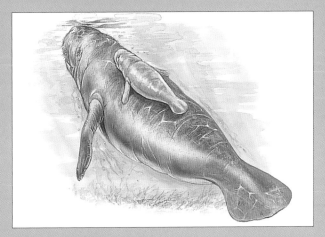

Although the calf can swim immediately, the mother will often give her newborn a lift to the surface for its first gulps of air.

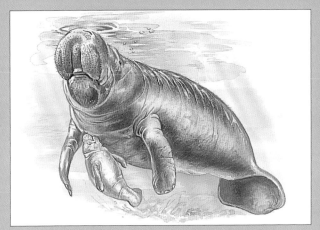

The calf will be dependent on its mother for one to two years, suckling milk from a nipple beneath her flipper.

Wolverine

It is known as the devil bear, skunk bear and 'kee-wa-har-kess' – 'the evil one'. With a reputation as a pest and a glutton, the misunderstood wolverine is now struggling for survival.

Coat
Wolverines have long been hunted by indigenous people, as their thick, glossy brown fur is valued as a lining for clothing.

Feet

Wolverines' short legs are tipped with broad feet and five, clawed toes. These are useful in hunting, but also prevent them from slipping on the ice. Most animals walk on their toes, but, like bears, wolverines have a plantigrade gape, which means that they put their entire foot on the ground to get a better grip on the surface.

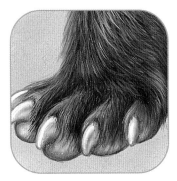

Key Facts	ORDER *Carnivora* / FAMILY *Mustelidae* GENUS & SPECIES *Gulo gulo*
Weight	7–34kg (15–75lb)
Length Head and body Tail	66–104cm (26–41in) 16.5–25cm (6.5–10in)
Sexual maturity	2–3 years
Mating season	Late April to July
Gestation period	About 9 months, including time for delayed implantation
Number of young	1–5, usually 2–4
Birth interval	2–3 years
Typical diet	Carrion, birds and their eggs, lemmings, wild sheep, caribou, nuts, fruit
Life span	Up to 17 years in captivity; 13 in the wild

Head

The heavy, bearlike head is unusual for a member of the weasel family, which typically have slender, 'triangular' features.

Jaws

Powerful, muscular jaws mean that the wolverine can bite down with (literally) bone-crunching force on its prey.

Wolverine habitats

The worst offenders of the family are striped skunks (*Mephitis mephitis*), which can famously spray their foul stench up to 3m (9ft 10in). Wolverines can manage only 1m (3ft 3in), but their spray is equally potent. The purpose of such apparently antisocial behaviour is twofold. First, it is believed that wolverines communicate with members of their species through sound and scent – marking their territory and advertising their availability to mate through complex chemical signals in their urine and musk glands. Secondly, it is a defence mechanism. Wolverines are wary in the presence of humans and will often raise their tail as a warning that a chemical attack is about to be unleashed.

melly, fierce and cunning it may be, but the wolverine does not deserve its bad reputation. These stocky mammals are also one of the Arctic's great predators, able to swim, climb and track prey over vast distances.

Chemical Weapons

The wolverine – or 'glutton', as it is known – is the largest and fiercest terrestrial member of the weasel family, Mustelidae. Members of this group are typically long-bodied and short-legged, with thick fur. Wolverines of both the Old and New World (*Gulo gulo gulo* and *Gulo gulo luscus*) tend to be stockier and more bearlike than weasels or skunks, but they share their ability to emit a potent, malodorous vapour from their anal glands.

Home on the Range

Life in the Arctic can be tough, as food is scarce. So a large territory – up to 920 square kilometres (572 square miles) – is important in order to get enough to eat. Generally, male wolverines are solitary, but they share their range with several females with whom they mate. Resources are not sufficient for them to breed every year, but, when they do, females are able to use a process called 'delayed implantation' to ensure that the young are born at just the right time. Wolverines typically mate between June and July, but it can be up to six months before the fertilized

Comparisons

Wolverines, in common with other members of the weasel family, carry their head and tail lower than their arched back, which gives them an uneven and slightly lumbering gait. Yet, like all weasels, wolverines are capable of remarkable speed and agility, especially when in pursuit of prey.

Sea otter   Wolverine   American marten   Least weasel

ovum (egg cell) attaches itself to the uterus, where the baby begins to develop. It will be ten more weeks before the young, white furred 'kits' are weaned. During this time, males often help to rear the young, and will travel up to 50km (31 miles) a night through their range to ensure that there is enough food for all.

Threats and Conservation

Wolverines have a 'circumpolar' distribution which means that their home ranges can be found along the Northern, temperate to sub-arctic hemisphere, in a broad band that stretches from Alaska in the United States and across Canada to Russia, Eastern Europe and into Scandinavia and Greenland. Historically, though, this capable predator was much more widespread. Michigan, for example,

is known as the wolverine state because they were once so plentiful in the region.

As people move into their traditional territories, wolverines are being forced to migrate further and further north. In Europe, where there are few areas of real wilderness left, this has brought them into conflict with the local population, which views them as pests. In the United States, too, wolverines are frequently shot and have little legal protection. They are listed as 'Vulnerable' by the IUCN, but more information is needed about this reclusive species before a workable conservation plan can be drawn up and put into action. Organizations such as the Wolverine Foundation are making a good start by changing people's attitude to this tenacious and intelligent Arctic survivor.

Wolverines will eat almost anything, but a fresh meal of caribou is a welcome addition to the menu.

With broad feet, which act like snowshoes, the wolverine is able to move through icy terrain with ease.

An animal ten times its size is no problem for the wolverine, which attacks the caribou by powerful slashing and ripping bites to the throat and head.

What it cannot eat in one sitting will be saved for later, as the wolverine's bone-crushing jaws have no trouble crunching through frozen meat.

144

CENTRAL
AMERICA

CARIBBEAN SEA

Amazon
Basin

SOUTH
AMERICA

Andes

SOUTH PACIFIC
OCEAN

Pampas

Patagonia

SOUTH
ATLANTIC
OCEAN

South and Central America

Mexico, Central and South America, and the islands of the West Indies, together comprise a rich and diverse region known collectively as Latin America. Here you will find bustling metal and glass cities, snow-laden mountains, sweeping deserts, vast rainforests and a greater variety of plants and animals than anywhere else on the planet.

At the heart of this tear-shaped landmass is the Amazon rainforest. Biologist Norman Myers has called rainforests 'the finest celebration of nature ever known', and these are places that have been described as 'the richest, oldest, most productive and most complex ecosystems on Earth'. Home to a quarter of the world's animals, this region of incredible abundance is also one of the most threatened. In the time it takes to read this paragraph, 60 hectares (149 acres) of rainforest will have been destroyed, much of this to feed the world's demand for wood, oil, minerals and beef. At the current rate of deforestation, it is believed that Latin America's great green lungs will completely cease to exist by 2030, with catastophric effects for the rest of the world. As the forests vanish, so, too, do around 137 species every day.

Deforestation is not the only problem facing this region's spectacular wildlife. Pollution, climate change, desertification, hunting and introduced species are all taking their toll. It is a problem that is no longer just the concern of one nation. Species exist here that are found nowhere else on the planet, making the conservation of Latin America's wildlife of global importance.

Long-tailed Chinchilla

With their luxurious fur, large, black eyes and intelligent gaze, long-tailed chinchillas are a popular household pet. In their arid Andean homelands, however, fewer than 10,000 individuals now remain.

Hind feet

When eating, long-tailed chinchillas sit back on their long, padded feet. These keep the chinchillas steady while they grasp their food with their tiny forearms.

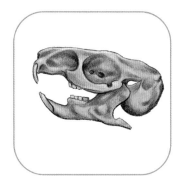

Teeth

Chinchillas are rodents. In common with all members of this group, they have teeth that grow constantly. These have enamel only on the front, and not the back, which means that over time they become worn into the shape of a chisel.

Key Facts	ORDER *Rodentia* / FAMILY *Chinchillidae* GENUS & SPECIES *Chinchilla laniger, Chinchilla brevicaudata*	
Weight	Male up to 500g (18oz); female up to 800g (28oz)	
Length Head and body Tail	22.5–38cm (8.8–15in) 7.5–15cm (3–6in)	
Sexual maturity	8 months	
Mating season	May–November	
Gestation period	110 days	
Number of young	2–6	
Birth interval	6 months	
Typical diet	Grass and herbs	
Life span	Up to 20 years in captivity; about 10 years in the wild	

Whiskers
Long, thin whiskers are
touch-sensitive. These help
the chinchilla to find its
way around in the dark.

Comparisons

Chinchillas and viscachas (*Lagidium viscacia*) are the only members of the family Chinchillidae. Both of these gregarious rodents can be found in the mountainous, rugged, uphill regions of the Andes. Larger than the long-tailed chinchilla, viscachas have similar habits to rabbits and build underground burrows, from which they emerge at sunset to bask and play.

Chinchilla

Mountain viscacha

There are believed to be two species of chinchilla – the long-tailed and the short-tailed, *Chinchilla brevicaudata*. *Chinchilla brevicaudata* are believed to be extinct in the wild, while their long-tailed relatives are currently listed as 'Vulnerable' by the IUCN.

A Big Softie

Living in the mountains of Chile, at 3000–5000m (9842–16,404 ft) above sea level, the long-tailed chinchilla must be able to keep warm. That is why this small rodent has such fabulously thick fur. In fact, chinchilla fur is so dense that parasites such as fleas are unable to live in it. We humans have just one hair for every hair follicle, but chinchillas have 50–60 hairs. That adds up to around 20,000 hairs per square centimetre (0.15 square inch) of fur. This fabulous fur is also 30 times softer than human hair, making their coats the softest and densest of any living animal.

To keep this fleece in tiptop condition, chinchillas need to have regular dust baths. This removes any excess oil that builds up. On no account should a chinchilla's fur be moistened, as this only tangles the hair. In nature, this spectacular coat is a striking pearl-grey colour, but chinchillas have been kept for years as pets and selectively bred. This means that white, beige, black and violet variations also exist in captivity.

The Call of the Wild

Young long-tailed chinchillas are born, in litters of two to six, between May and November. During this time, the female chinchilla may become extremely aggressive, but this is unusual. In general, chinchillas are an extremely sociable species and groups live together in huge colonies. In the past, such colonies could number as much as a hundred individuals; however, with their population declining, groups today are typically much smaller.

Chinchilla habitat

Nestled in holes among the rocks keeps the long-tailed chinchillas safe from predators such as birds of prey.

Although primarily nocturnal, individuals may occasionally come out in the late afternoon to bask in the warm sun.

A dust bath is an essential part of the chinchilla's routine, removing unwanted moisture from the fur. This helps to keep its insulating properties.

Strong hind legs, padded 'non-slip' feet and a long tail for balance allow chinchillas to perform impressive acrobatics.

Chinchillas can live for up to 15 years in captivity, and during this time they form strong bonds with other colony members, keeping in constant contact with one other through a range of calls. Chinchillas have an extremely wide aural range, which is believed to be similar to that of a human's. A quite chirruping, for example, may mean that the chinchilla is curious, as this is a noise often heard in captive Long-tailed Chinchillas when they've been introduced to a new environment. They've even been known to sneeze and grind their teeth! Their most aggressive call is a high, loud bark, which warns the colony that danger is near.

Threats and Conservation
Like the Vicuña, Long-tailed Chinchillas have long been valued for their meat and soft fur. This trade dates back to the sixteenth century, when European conquistadors arrived in the Americas. By the 1900s, around 500,000 chinchilla skins were exported from Chile every year to make luxury fur coats. As 150 chinchilla pelts were used for every coat, this meant that 3333 garments were made for every half a million animals killed. At one point, the market value for just one pelt was US $100,000!

It goes without saying that no species can stand such an onslaught forever. Over the centuries, chinchillas have retreated further and further into the arid and isolated mountain regions, where they are relatively safe from hunters. Now these beleaguered survivors are faced by a new threat: habitat loss. So far, reintroducing species from captive stock has not been successful, and more information is urgently needed about their lifestyles. Sadly, these shy and appealing mammals may soon be extinct.

Flightless Cormorant

Although this species is flightless, it still retains recognizable, if scruffy, wings. With blackish feathers and a raucous, growling call, these unique marine birds are restricted to just two islands in the Galapagos range: Fernandia and Isabela.

Throat sac

Cormorants are very vocal, thanks to a small throat sac (A). This acts like an echo chamber, expanding whenever the cormorant cries out (B).

A   B

Key Facts	ORDER *Pelecaniformes* / FAMILY *Phalacrocorcidae* GENUS & SPECIES *Phalacrocorax harrisi*
Weight	2.5–4kg (5.5–9lb)
Length	89–101cm (35–40in)
Sexual maturity	2 years
Breeding season	All year, but mainly March–September
Number of eggs	1–4; usually 2 or 3
Incubation period	About 35 days
Fledging period	About 60 days
Breeding interval	Usually 1 year, but may breed twice per year
Typical diet	Fish, eels, squid and octopus
Life span	Unknown

Wings

Like the flippers of the macaroni penguin, these short and narrow wings are no use for flying – or even swimming. Instead, the cormorant relies on its powerful webbed feet to power through the water.

Feet

Like all cormorants, *Phalacrocorax harrissi* has webbed feet. These make the bird ungainly on land, but provide excellent propulsion when diving and swimming.

Flightless cormorants are sometimes called Galapagos cormorants because they make their homes in the Archipiélago de Colón off the coast of Ecuador – a group of islands that are commonly called the Galapagos.

Home, Sweet Home

Flightless cormorants are real home bodies. These unique birds inhabit rocky shores, building nests with twigs, seaweed and other flotsam, just above the waterline. Living in small breeding colonies of around 12 pairs of birds, they

Flightless cormorant habitats

rarely move more than 1000m (1096yd) from their breeding grounds during their entire lives.

The climate in this region is relatively mild, and there are few predators and plenty of food, which is probably why the ancestors of today's Galapagos cormorants lost their ability to fly. They simply did not need to. Instead, this marine bird has become a skilled swimmer, able to make dives and pursue prey through the water with remarkable speed. Cormorant feathers are not waterproof, however, so the birds dry them out by basking in the sun. As they do so, they hold their stubby wings out at an angle. Amazingly, all cormorants – even those in zoos, where they do not have to dive for food – dry their wings in exactly the same way after feeding.

The Enchanted Isle

Throughout history, the Galapagos Islands have been places of myth and legend. They were once called the Enchanted Isles because it was believed that pirates used to bury their stolen treasure there. Their Spanish name, Galápagos, is taken from the name given to the giant tortoises that made the islands famous. Yet, these giant shelled reptiles are not the island's only strange and spectacular inhabitants. There are numerous unique species here, including the marine iguana (*Amblyrhynchus cristatus*) and five sea birds – the flightless cormorant, the Galapagos penguin (*Spheniscus mendiculus*), the waved albatross (*Diomedea irrorata*), the swallow-tailed gull (*Creagrus furcata*) and the dusky gull (*Larus fuliginosus*). It was unique species

Comparisons

Guanay cormorants (*Phalacrocorax bougainvillii*) are much more widespread than their Galapagos relatives. Found on both the Pacific and Atlantic coasts of Latin America, these smaller members of the family Phalacrocoracidae can fly, but, like the Galapagos cormorants, live an almost entirely marine life.

Flightless cormorant

Guanay cormorant

such as these which naturalist Charles Darwin (1809–1882) studied in 1835, while developing his revolutionary theories about evolution. By examining species in other parts of Latin America, and comparing them to those he found in the Galapagos, Darwin could see that those in the islands were different. They had changed (or 'evolved') in response to their environment.

Threats and Conservation

Hunted, preyed on by introduced species, caught in fishermen's nets and poisoned by oil slicks, flightless cormorants have struggled to survive over the centuries. Within the Galapagos National Park and Maritime Reserve, cormorants now have the full protection of the law, but nothing can protect them from chance. A graphic example of this was seen when El Niño hit the Galapagos

in 1983. This warm current can completely change the ecosystem of a region by wiping out local marine species and attracting temporary invaders. This El Niño was equally destructive, and killed half of the island's cormorant population.

Cormorants are practical parents. They breed from July to October, when food is plentiful. In times of excess, the females will leave their mates to raise one set of large, shaggy chicks and go off to establish another nest with a second male. After the disaster of El Niño, the cormorant population fell to just 400 individuals, but, with extra food for the survivors, breeding adults quickly re-established the population. The cormorants were lucky, but with such a restricted range, extreme changes in climate, outbreaks of disease and environmental disasters still have the capacity to do irrevocable damage.

Flightless cormorants are aquatic predators, able to swim with great agility in search of a favourite meal.

Propelled by their large webbed feet, cormorants can dive and change direction quickly when in pursuit of prey.

Their long, hooked bills help cormorants to catch, hold and manipulate prey such as octopus, squid or eel.

Most meals can be swallowed whole. Indigestible parts, such as bones, are then regurgitated later.

Giant Otter

The presence of giant otters has long been used to track the environmental health of a region. As Latin America's clean rivers vanish — polluted by industry and mining — so, too, have populations of this swift and appealing semi-aquatic mammal.

Whiskers

Stiff, sensitive whiskers, similar to those worn by seals, help the giant otter to detect its prey in the dark, murky waters of the Amazon Basin's rivers.

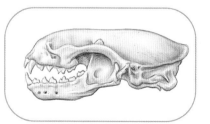

Skull

The slightly flattened, streamlined skull of this mammal tells us all we need to know — that these intelligent and agile creatures spend much of their time in the water.

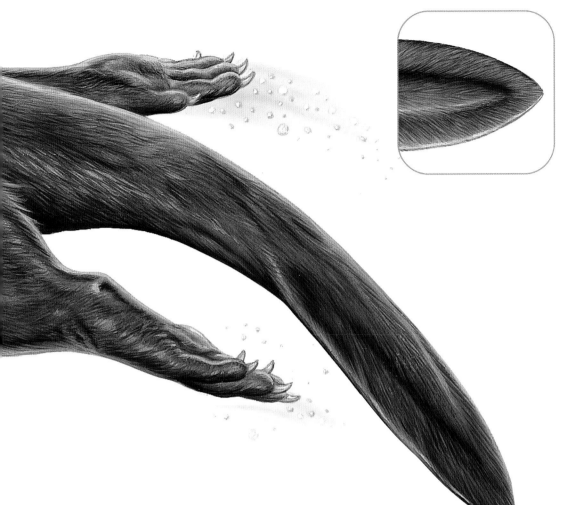

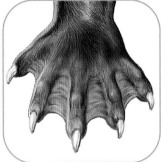

Tail

This Latin American giant has a broad, paddle-shaped tail, with 'flanges' along the edges. This gives the otter additional thrust when swimming.

Feet

The giant otter's huge feet have five clawed toes. These are webbed, which helps this sleek, muscular mammal to propel itself through the water.

Key Facts

ORDER *Carnivora* / FAMILY *Mustelidae* / GENUS & SPECIES *Pteronura brasiliensis*

Weight	Male 26–34kg (57–75lb); female 22–26kg (49–57lb)
Length Head and body Tail	Male 1–1.4m (3ft 3in–4 ft 6in); female 0.9–1.1m (2ft 11in–3ft 7in) Male 50–60cm (20–24in); female 45–50cm (17.7–20in)
Sexual maturity	2 years
Mating season	All year
Gestation period	52–79 days
Number of young	1–5, but usually 2
Birth interval	About 9 months
Typical diet	Mainly fish, crabs and frogs; occasionally larger prey such as snakes and caimans
Life span	Unknown

Comparisons

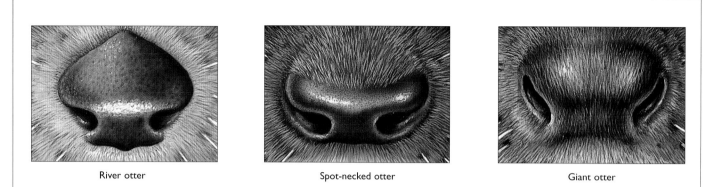

River otter   Spot-necked otter   Giant otter

Despite their differences in size and habitat, all otters share the same basic body shape: long, sleek bodies; a flattened head; tiny, almost residual ears; webbed feet; and a broad tail.

In fact, the only way to identify each species is from tiny differences. Giant Otters have broad, furry nose pads. African Spot-necked Otters (*Hydrictis maculicollis*) have wider, hairless noses, while the nose of the River Otter (*Lutra canadensis*) resembles that of a bear.

Despite their prowess in the water, otters are members of the cosmopolitan family Mustelidae, which includes many purely terrestrial species, such as black-footed ferrets, wolverines, weasels and badgers.

Water Babies
Giant otters, known locally as 'river wolves', are endemic to the rivers and rainforests of Latin America. They inhabit lakes, swamps and wetlands, their ideal environment being

Giant otter habitats

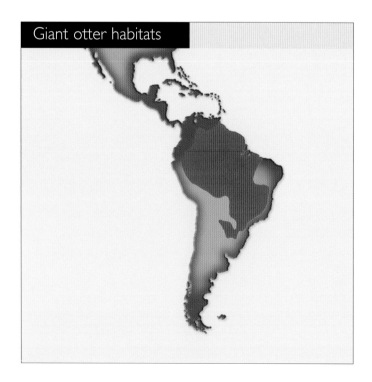

slow-running water, such as the region's famous 'blackwaters'. Despite their name, these waterways are not polluted, but simply stained by rotting leaves and debris from the forest. These waterways are often full of submerged logs and underwater obstructions, which may be one of the reasons that they are favoured by otters. They are dark and hard to navigate, which are ideal conditions for hunting if you possess the aquatic skills of a giant otter.

These muscular mammals are relatively slow on land, but once in the water they are genuine acrobats. With their streamlined shape, large webbed feet and paddle-shaped tails, giant otters can manoeuvre through the tangle of submerged rainforest with ease. Such skills do not come easy. Young otter cubs begin their training at around three weeks old, when they begin to practise in the shallows. It can be four months, however, before they are able to swim confidently with the rest of the family.

Tight Knit
Giant otters live in small family groups called 'holts'. These are tightknit communities of between three and nine individuals, including two adults and their young kits.

Giant otters pair for life and breed throughout the year, although usually only one or two kits out of a litter of up to five will survive. Juveniles may stay with the holt for two years and will take it in turns to help look after the latest additions to the family. Mum is the head of this little group, and she takes the kits out of the communal riverside den to feed in the early morning and afternoon.

Here she will teach them how to catch their favourite food – fish. Adult giant otters have no natural predators, apart from man, but their kits are vulnerable to attacks from anacondas and caimans, so both parents make regular patrols of the river and will actively harass any predators in their territory.

Threats and Conservation

These huge, sleek mammals are found only in clean, unpolluted and undisturbed waterways. They do not make their homes anywhere else. This means that not only do we know that a river is pure because there are otters living there, but we can also track the spread of pollution by their absence. Gold mining takes place in the Amazon Basin on a massive scale, involving 1.2 million people spread over 170,000 square kilometres (65,637 square miles). The loss of so many otters in recent decades shows how the waters of the Amazon Basin have become contaminated by the polluted runoff from such mines. Mercury poisoning is especially problematic because, even if the otters themselves live in uncontaminated waters, their food is being slowly poisoned.

Boat traffic, oil spills and conflicts with local fisherman (who believe that the otters take their catches) are also depleting populations. These beautiful mammals are legally protected from hunters and poachers, but anti-pollution legislation has been slower to arrive and the future of the giant otter is uncertain.

Giant otters build dens on gently sloping sections of the river bank. This allows them to slip in and out of the water quickly and easily.

When hunting, giant otters either follow the fish, matching their speed and direction exactly, or dive and lie in wait for a meal to approach.

Otters need to breathe air, so they must surface regularly. After the hunt, they will head for the bank with their successful catch.

The giant otter's powerful jaws allow them to eat fish whole, as they are able to crunch up their prey's bones and scales with their sharp teeth.

Golden Lion Tamarin

The first European to document the golden lion tamarin was the Italian navigator Antonio Pigafetta (1491–1535), who described them as 'beautiful, simian-like cats similar to small lions'. Today, these golden lion tamarins have become the pin-ups of the conservation world.

Teeth

Golden lion tamarins are omnivores – as shown by their teeth. Long, sharp canines are used to tear at food, while flat molars help to reduce fruit to a pulp.

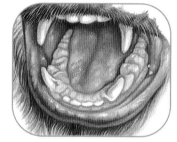

Key Facts	ORDER *Primates* / FAMILY *Callitrichidae*
	GENUS & SPECIES *Leontopithecus rosalia*

Weight	600–800g (21–28oz)
Length Head and body Tail	20–34cm (8–13in) 32–40cm (12.5–15.7in)
Sexual maturity	Male 2 years; female 18 months
Mating season	Spring to autumn
Gestation period	125–132 days
Number of young	Almost always gives birth to twins
Breeding interval	One litter per year; two if the first litter dies
Typical diet	Fruit, insects, spiders, small vertebrates, gum, sap and resin
Life span	About 15 years in captivity; 5–8 years in the wild

Tail

Lion Tamarins, like Old World monkeys, do not have prehensile (or grasping) tails. Instead, their tails help them to keep their balance when scrambling among the rainforest canopy.

Claws

Four of the tamarin's five front and rear claws
are tipped with long, curved nails — a feature
unusual in Latin American monkeys. These help
the tamarins to forage for insects and grubs.

Golden Lion Tamarin habitats

There are 14 species of tamarin in the family Callitrichidae. All of them make their homes in the rapidly vanishing forests of Latin America.

Communal Living

Most tamarins are brightly coloured, with red, brown or white fur. Some, such as the emperor tamarin (*Saguinus imperator*), have white, showy, drooping moustaches. Others have flowing, silken fur on their heads, but Brazil's golden lion tamarin is the most famous of all. These little primates have long, glowing, golden coats and fine, silky manes that frame their small, round faces.

To keep these stunning coats in tiptop condition, tamarins regularly groom one another. This is a practice common to most primates – monkeys and apes – and is an important way for colony members to bond with the rest of the group. Tamarin societies tend to be small and tightknit, comprised of two adults and their offspring (up to eight members). These groups also share food and baby-sitting responsibilities, so good relationships, bolstered by close physical contact, are important.

Threats

Golden lion tamarins are arboreal, and make their homes in tropical rainforests along Brazil's Atlantic coast. These attractive monkeys hunt by day, relying on vines and heavy foliage to provide them with a natural corridor through the forest, safe from predators. At night, they sleep in the holes in tree trunks or use the large rosette-shaped, fleshy leaves of bromeliads as nests.

A staggering 90 per cent of the tamarin's traditional habitats has now vanished, as forests are cut down to make way for cattle farming and development. The effect on tamarin populations has been nothing short of catastrophic. By 1990, there were fewer than 100 of these gentle monkeys left in the wild, and they were considered to be 'Critically Endangered' by the IUCN. Fortunately, almost 30 years of conservation work has brought this appealing forest dweller back from the brink.

Each tamarin colony is founded by a breeding pair, which stays together for life and shares the responsibility for raising the young.

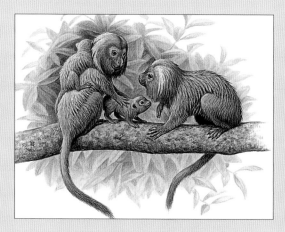

Twins are almost always born. These are usually carried on the father's back, but are handed over to the mother every few hours for feeding.

Comparisons

Golden lion tamarins are closely related to marmosets, both of which belong to the family Callithricidae. While tamarins enjoy a broad omnivorous diet, pygmy marmosets (*Callithrix pygmaea*) feed mainly on the sap from gum trees. To aid this process, their very large, sharp incisor teeth point forwards, so that they can be used to gouge holes in the tree trunks.

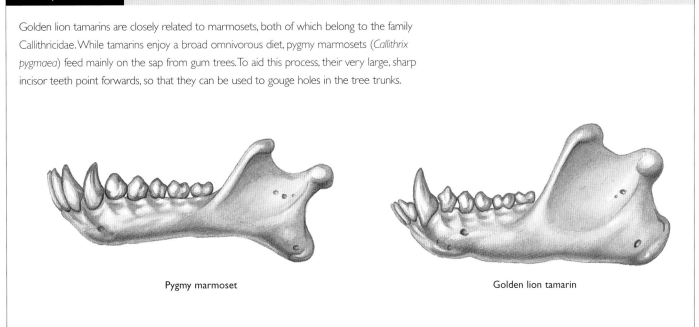

Pygmy marmoset   Golden lion tamarin

Conservation

In 2004, the IUCN reassessed the status of the golden lion tamarin and decided that conservation efforts were sufficient to reclassify the species as 'Endangered'.

There are still fewer than 1000 individuals left in the wild. That is not enough to be considered secure, but the rise in numbers does show how useful captive breeding programmes can be, as almost one-third were born in zoos. These populations are currently divided between 17 areas along the coast. There is no forest to link these regions, so each colony is isolated – a situation that, it is hoped, can be rectified by reforesting areas to provide wildlife corridors. Some populations have also been relocated to a new protected zone, the União Biological Reserve. Here they are safe from hunters and poachers, although not natural predators, as was discovered recently when a weasel-like predator called the tayra (*Eira barbara*), learned how to break into tamarin nests. Given that there are so few tamarins left, natural events such as this can be disastrous; however, their continued survival in the face of difficult odds has made this golden monkey a beacon for conservation movements worldwide.

The pair will suckle for up to half an hour before they are handed back to their father or another member of the colony.

Juvenile members of the group do not breed, but they practise their parenting skills on the new babies, carefully grooming and carrying them.

Macaroni Penguin

In the eigtheenth century, a 'macaroni' was a type of
English dandy who wore feathers in his hat – just
like in the famous song 'Yankee Doodle'. This
is where the increasingly vulnerable,
golden-crested macaroni penguins
get their rather curious name.

Key Facts	ORDER *Sphenisciformes* FAMILY *Spheniscidae* GENUS & SPECIES *Eudyptes chrysolophus*
Weight	4.9–5.8kg (11–13lb)
Height	71cm (28in)
Sexual maturity	Female 5 years; male 6 years
Breeding season	October–December
Number of eggs	2, with only 1 surviving
Incubation period	60–70 days
Fledging period	2 years
Typical diet	Fish, squid, crustaceans, and krill
Life span	Unknown

Chick

Macaroni penguin chicks lack
their parent's elegant yellow
crests. These emerge only after
two years. Their bills, too, are
less dramatic than they are in
adulthood, being dark brown,
rather than red.

Feet

The soles of the macaroni
penguin are black. Dark colours
absorb heat, so this helps to
keep the penguin warm.

Flippers

Penguins are members of the bird family, but, instead of traditional wings, a pair of stiff flippers are used to propel them through the water.

Bill

The lower part of the macaroni penguin's bill is ridged. This helps to give the penguin a better grip on its prey.

Penguins belong to a separate group of flightless birds known as the order Sphenisciformes. Completely at home in the ocean, this remarkable species is the most marine of all birds.

Bizarre Birds

Penguins are perhaps the oddest members of the bird group. Completely flightless, these stocky Southern Hemisphere inhabitants have short, thick feathers, which are white on their bellies and black on their backs, making them look a little like overweight butlers. Their stubby legs are almost invisible beneath layers of thick, insulating blubber. Just their pink webbed feet stick out. A pair of stiff flippers and, in the case of the macaroni penguin, a crest of what looks like overgrown yellow eyebrows complete the outfit.

Comical though it looks, this odd design makes penguins excellent swimmers. Instead of flight feathers, the macaroni's dense plumage makes this bizarre bird almost completely waterproof. Flippers help to propel it through the water, while its large feet act like rudders to control direction. Indeed, these birds are such accomplished swimmers that outside of the breeding season they are believed to be wholly pelagic. In other words, they have no permanent roosts, but live entirely in the open ocean.

Two Heads Better Than One

Macaroni penguins may spend much of the year at sea, but, once mating season arrives in October, they head for favoured breeding sites, on rocky islands within the South Atlantic, off the coasts of Argentina, Brazil and Chile. Penguins mate for life and, once they have reached dry

Penguin colonies (which are called rookeries) can contain as many as a million individuals, tightly packed into a small nesting area.

Although they have a high tolerance for their neighbours, the birds follow well-trodden routes in and out of the colony to avoid conflict.

When conflict does flare up, opponents trumpet loudly and lock bills in a joust, where the aim is to force the intruder to the ground.

Penguins are highly vocal, and once back at the nest they replace aggressive calls with an affectionate chattering as the breeding pair prepare to change shifts.

land, they greet their partners with excited trumpeting calls, much head shaking and bowing. Reunion over, they then begin the task of constructing a nest from mud and gravel, which they line with stones.

Macaronis, like most penguins, lay two eggs, around five days apart. The first egg is usually smaller than the second and is quickly discarded. Unusually in the animal kingdom, both parents take shifts incubating the egg and hunting for food until, four to five weeks later, it hatches. Then the arduous task of caring for and feeding the rapidly growing chick begins. Again, the task is divided equally between the male and female. For four weeks, until the chick can be left in the colony 'nursery', the male will guard the nest while the female hunts for food.

Threats and Conservation

The macaroni penguin is generally believed to be one of the most numerous penguins in the world. With nine million breeding pairs worldwide, its future seems secure. So why is this apparently abundant species considered to be 'Vulnerable' by the IUCN? The justification lies in the fact that the population has declined by 30 per cent in just three generations. Statistics may be misleading, but such a sudden drop in the numbers of a previously 'healthy' species is cause for concern.

Penguins have few natural predators, apart from sea lions and killer whales. With species numbers so high, hunting

Macaroni penguin habitats

by humans is not believed to be a major problem either. The real threat is pollution, and the amount of oil, heavy metals and toxins that are beginning to filter into the penguin's food chain. More research on this is needed before it can be determined if the macaroni penguin is truly in trouble, but history has shown us that even the most plentiful species need our constant care.

Comparisons

Although similar in appearance to the royal penguin (*Eudyptes schlegeli*), the macaroni is the largest of the six species of crested penguins belonging to the genus *Eudyptes*. They also usually have black faces and a broad, bulbous bill. Royal penguins, in comparison, have white faces and narrower bills.

Royal penguin

Macaroni penguin

Spectacled Bear

Despite their relatively small size, spectacled bears have the distinction of being one of Latin America's largest carnivores, and the region's only bear. This shy and reclusive species is rarely been seen outside zoos, where they are a popular attraction.

Spectacles
The circles of cream-coloured fur forming distinct rings around this small bear's eyes, like a pair of glasses, are the reason for its unusual name. This pale fur may also extend down the neck and chest.

Key Facts	ORDER *Carnivora* / FAMILY *Ursidae* / GENUS & SPECIES *Tremarctos ornatus*
Weight	Male 100–170kg (220–375lb); female 60–90kg (132–198lb)
Length Head and body Tail	 1.2–1.8m (3ft 11in–5ft 11in) 7cm (2.75in)
Shoulder height	70–80cm (27.5–31.5in)
Sexual maturity	Male unknown, probably 5–6 years; female 4–7 years
Mating season	April–June
Gestation period	195–255 days
Number of young	1–3
Breeding interval	2 years
Typical diet	Fruit and other vegetation; some animal matter
Life span	Up to 36 years in captivity, 20 years in the wild

Body
Spectacled bears are sexually dimorphic: males and females are physically different from each other. An adult male may weigh up to 50 per cent more then his female counterpart, and be one-third larger.

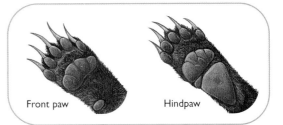

Front paw   Hindpaw

Feet

Unusually for bears, this species spends much of its time in the tree tops. Spectacled bears are proficient climbers, thanks to their furry paws and long, sharp claws, which help them to keep their grip on the tree trunk as they ascend.

Spectacled bear habitats

Compact in size, with a thick neck, rounded head and short snout, the spectacled bear is one of the smaller and stockier members of the bear family, Ursidae.

A Rare Spectacle

Little is known about the habits of the spectacled bear in the wild, as they tend to inhabit isolated regions of the Andes mountain range, at 1800–2700m (5900–8860ft) above sea level.

Generally nocturnal, these stocky bears forage for food between dusk and dawn. In common with other members of this diverse family, spectacled bears are believed to be omnivores, which means that they eat a wide range of foods, from small mammals and birds to berries. However, they seem to be primarily herbivorous, their favourite foods are fruits and Bromeliads. They eat the leaves, bases and hearts of Bromeliads, and build treetop platforms where they can lie and gorge themselves on the season's freshest offerings, in between naps. Spectacled bears generally only inhabit regions where these particular delicacies are abundant.

Fame and Fortune

In the past, local Andean tribes people revered the spectacled bear, believing that it had mystical and magical properties. Many stories were told about this most iconic of Latin American animals, including one tale that describes how a spectacled bear took a beautiful village woman to be his wife. Together, the pair made a home in the tree tops, and after many years the woman eventually gave birth to a son. This child was half-man and half-bear, but came to reject his animal nature. Killing his father, the son eventually returned with his mother to her village.

Today, the spectacled bear is still considered to be precious, but for far more sinister reasons. Bear gall bladders are used as an ingredient in oriental medicines,

Comparisons

The sloth bear (*Ursus ursinus*) is the Indian subcontinent's answer to the spectacled bear. Both of these species are small and squat, with longer forelegs than back legs, which gives them a rolling, almost comical gait when they walk. Unlike the spectacled bear, however, whose small, bulbous snout has earned it the nickname of 'short-faced bear', the sloth bear has a long, narrow nose. As this species feeds primarily on insects, its snout works like a long tube, sucking up a meal of ants with an audible snuffle.

Sloth bear

Spectacled bear

and just one can fetch as much as US $150 on the black market. This may not sound much, but it represents five times the average monthly wage in Ecuador. A dead spectacled bear is thus a very valuable commodity indeed.

Threats and Conservation

Spectacled bears are listed on Appendix 1 of the Convention on International Trade in Endangered Species (CITES). This makes it illegal for anyone to trade in spectacled bears, their fur or their body parts. The problem is enforcing such a law in the vast, inaccessible mountain regions where the bears make their home.

Conservationists also face problems. A captive breeding programme is under way, but so little is known about this species that more information is needed before effective measures can be put into place. In the meantime, organizations such as the World Wide Fund for Nature (WWF) are working to find ways to eradicate hunting, and to identify suitable sites for nature reserves. For many species, an inaccessible habitat equals safety, but for the spectacled bear it is their very elusiveness that is hampering efforts to save it. We do not even know for certain how many there are left in the wild, but estimates vary from 10,000 to 20,000.

Spectacled bears are an adaptable species, occupying a range of habitats from mountain forests to grasslands and arid scrub.

An excellent sense of smell enables this small bear to hunt out tasty treats such as the fruit of the desert cactus.

The bear's thick fur protects it from the cactus's spines, as it climbs to the top of the trunk.

Holding the fruit between its jaws, the bear returns to the ground to eat its prize in comfort.

Vicuña

There were once more than
1.5 million vicuñas running wild
across the dry scrubland of the
Andean slopes. These graceful
ancestors of the domestic alpaca are
still threatened, but their return from
the brink of extinction has given
hope to conservationists worldwide.

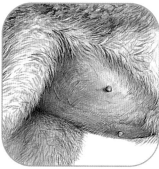

Nipples
During the breeding season,
teats supply the rapidly growing
young with a fresh supply of
nourishing milk.

Teeth
Like rodents, vicuñas have
lower teeth that grow
constantly. This prevents them
from becoming worn down
by the tough vegetation on
which the vicuñas graze.

Key Facts

ORDER *Artiodactyla* / **FAMILY** *Camelidae* / **GENUS & SPECIES** *Vicugna Vicugna*

Weight	35–65kg (77–143lb)
Length Head and body Tail	1.2–1.9m (3ft 11in–6ft 3in) 15–25cm (6–9.8in)
Shoulder height	70–110cm (27.5–43in)
Sexual maturity	2 years
Mating season	March–April
Gestation period	330–350 days
Number of young	1
Breeding interval	16 months
Typical diet	Coarse grasses
Life span	Up to 16 years in the wild; up to 24 years in captivity

Legs

When it wants to cool down, a vicuña will stand with its long, slender legs wide apart. This allows air to flow around its thighs, which have only a very thin covering of fur.

Vicuñas are the smallest members of the camel family, Camelidae. This is a group that includes the guanaco (*Lama guanicoe*) and the Bactrian camel (*Camelus bactrianus*).

Living on the Edge

Weighing as little as 35kg (77lb) and standing just 1.2m (3ft 11in) high, vicuñas may look slender and fragile, but are actually amazingly hardy.

On the high rocky grassland plateaux of the Andes mountain range, days can be scorching, with no trees to provide cover from the relentless rays of the sun. In the evening, the thin air quickly cools to freezing point. Water is scarce, and the only food for a vegetarian such as the vicuña is long, tough grasses called festuca.

Fortunately, vicuñas are ideally adapted to survive in such an extreme environment. Their teeth grow constantly, like those of rodents, so that they can eat the coarse vegetation without wearing them out. Their blood has an especially high red corpuscle count, which means that they can extract as much oxygen as possible from the thin mountain atmosphere. They walk on the tips of the fore and hind digits, but not their hooves, which allows them to use their two flexible toes to grip onto rocky slopes. The vicuñas' greatest weapon against such extremes, is their incredibly thick, soft coat. This traps hot air, to keep them warm in the evening, and shields their hide from the burning ultraviolet rays of the sun during the day.

Threats

Light and soft, with a shimmering lustre, vicuña wool was considered so precious by the ancient Incas that only the king and his court were allowed to wear it. Commoners could be executed simply for owning a shirt made of its fleece! To ensure that there was a constant supply of this wool, the Incas farmed these little camels, using a technique known as the '*chacu*'. This involved hundreds of people, who all worked together, to corral the vicuñas, so that their luxurious golden fleeces could then be shorn.

Vicuña habitats

Comparisons

Guanacos (*Lama guanicoe*) are the closest wild relative of the vicuña. Looking very much like long-necked sheep, guanacos can be found on both Andean slopes and plains. Their short, coarse hair is little use in clothing manufacture, which means that this large, red-brown species is currently more plentiful than its rare cousin.

Vicuña

Guanaco

Vicuñas live in family groups of between five and ten individuals, led by a dominant male. At adulthood, males leave the family to form bachelor groups of their own.

Each family group usually has two territories. The larger, feeding territory may cover as much as 18.2 hectares (45 acres). A smaller, more isolated territory is reserved for sleeping.

Vicuñas communicate using body signals and sounds. An 'orgling' noise is made to attract a mate, but raised ears, tail and a guttural rumble indicate a combative mood.

Food in the Andes is scarce, and the group cannot afford to share. If body signals and calls do not scare off an intruder, the dominant male will aggressively defend his territory.

Today, vicuña wool is still highly sought-after. In fact, it is the world's most valuable natural fibre, costing around US $225 per pound (450g). Yet, rather than corral these agile and graceful animals, poachers have, for decades, simply shot them – a brutal but faster and more effective way of cashing in on such a valuable 'crop'. By the late 1970s, poaching had reached such levels that vicuñas were close to extinction, with fewer than 8000 animals left in the wild.

Conservation

Alfonso Martinez is the man behind the vicuñas' amazing recovery. Having been raised in a mountain village, Martinez knew that it would take more than laws and legislation to stop the trade in vicuña wool. No one could expect a farmer who was struggling to feed his family to worry about conservation issues – particularly not when there was such a high bounty on a vicuña's head.

Traditionally, all vicuñas belonged to the state, but Martinez realized that if ownership of the camels and their fleece were handed over to the villagers, they would have a vested interest in keeping the animals safe. The next step was to take a leaf out of the books of the ancient Incas and revive the *chacu*, so that vicuñas could be shorn every two years. Already this innovative programme has saved the vicuña from extinction, and numbers are rising throughout its range. Once again, this graceful species is back where it belongs – in the wilds of the Andes.

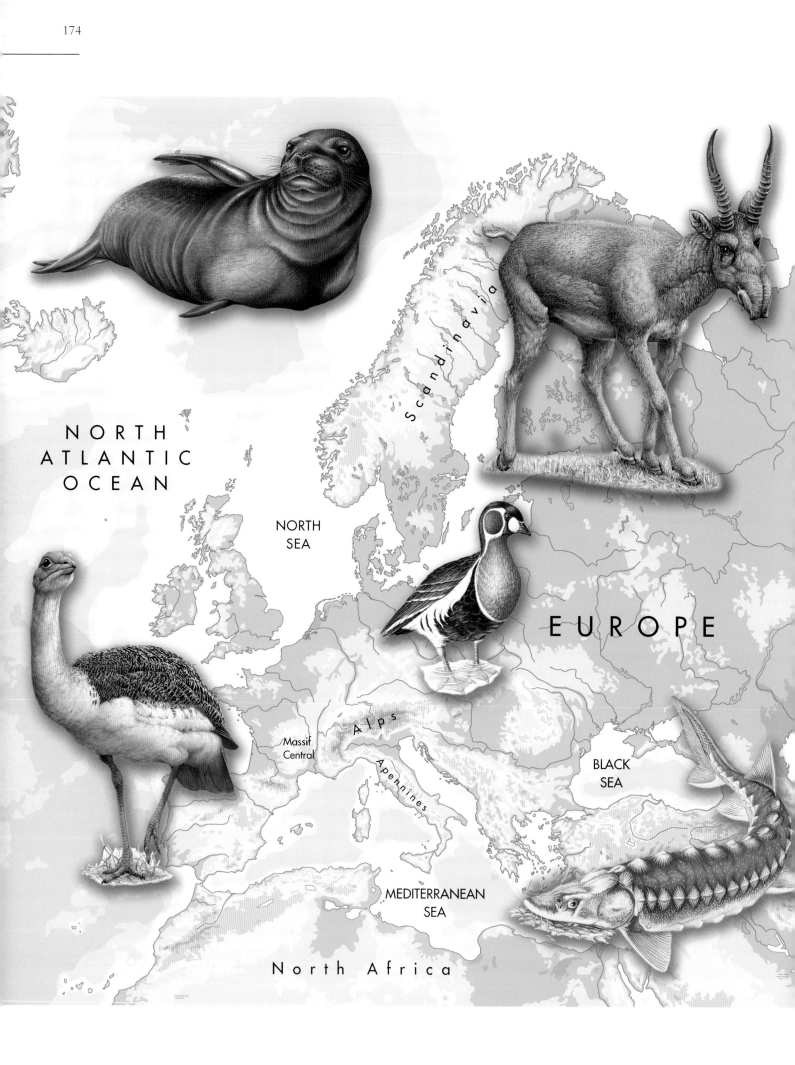

NORTH
ATLANTIC
OCEAN

NORTH
SEA

Scandinavia

EUROPE

Massif
Central

Alps

Apennines

BLACK
SEA

MEDITERRANEAN
SEA

North Africa

Europe

Europe is a vast peninsula that stretches across 14 time zones,
taking us from Iceland, in the heart of the wind-blown, grey Atlantic Ocean,
to the sweeping expanse of the Russian steppes. Within this cosmopolitan
region can be found a stunning range of wildlife habitats: the snowbound
Arctic tundra, the craggy Carpathian mountains, and the cold-water
coral reefs of the Atlantic oceans.

~

Bound together by common historical and cultural links, Europe is increasingly a political body, too, imposing blanket policies across the continent to the benefit or detriment of the environment. One of the most contentious of these has been the Common Agricultural Policy which, with its system of rewarding intensive farming methods, has helped almost to wipe out many common birds and mammals. With ten new member states joining the European Union in 2004, such policies could well spell disaster for many of the region's native species. But this is just a small part of the problem. Throughout the continent, vital habitats face destruction, such as 2.7 million hectares (6.7 million acres) of cork oak forest. As Europe's population grows, as her cities expand and as rural areas are turned over to farming and industry, the challenge for the people of this vibrant continent is how to find space for their rapidly vanishing natural treasures.

European Sturgeon

Caviar has been the downfall of these large, stout-bodied fish. Found primarily in the Northern Hemisphere, they have been declining in number for decades, due to the popularity of their eggs as a luxury food.

Scutes

Like a tortoise, the sturgeon has a body covered with bony plates called 'scutes'. The shape and number of scutes can be used to identify specific species.

Mouth

Sturgeons of the family Acipenser have no teeth. Instead, beneath a long snout is a downward-facing protrusile mouth that can be thrust forwards to suck up prey.

Key Facts	ORDER *Acipenseriformes* / FAMILY *Acipenseridae* GENUS & SPECIES *Acipenser sturio*
Weight	Up to 300kg (661lb)
Length	Male 1–1.5m (3ft 3in–4ft 11in); female 1.3–2m (4ft 3in–6ft 6in). Occasionally, both sexes may reach 3.5m (11ft 6in)
Sexual maturity	Male 7–9 years; female 8–14 years
Breeding season	Spring to early summer
Number of eggs	Up to 2.5 million, depending on size of female
Hatching interval	3–7 days
Breeding interval	1 year
Typical diet	Crustaceans, molluscs, insect larvae, worms and small fish
Life span	Unknown, but possibly 100 years or more

Barbels

Four slender bristles, called 'barbels', are used as sensitive feelers to help the sturgeons locate food as they push their long snouts through the mud and silt on the seabed.

There are 17 members of the order Acipenseriformes, 16 of which are currently listed as 'Vulnerable', 'Endangered' or 'Critically Endangered' by the IUCN. This list includes not just the European sea sturgeon (*Acipenser sturio*), but also species worldwide, including the Russian (*Acipenser gueldenstaedtii*), Chinese (*Acipenser sinensis*) and Persian (*Acipenser ruthenus*).

Old-fashioned Style

Sturgeons belong to an order of fish whose ancestors first appeared on Earth during the Jurassic Period, 180 million years ago. In common with other ancient fish, such as sharks, their skeletons are largely boneless, composed of an elastic substance called 'cartilage'. Their tail fins, too, follow a primitive pattern where their vertebrae turns upwards and extends out into a large, pointed lobe (a design called 'heterocercal'). Instead of scales, their slender bodies have bony scutes that run in rows, along the back and sides of the fish.

Their most unusual feature, however, is not visible because it is inside their bodies. Like sharks, the sturgeon has intestines with a specialized spiral valve, which effectively slows down the digestive system – forcing food in a spiral route through the gut gives the body more time to absorb nutrients from the food.

Heading Home

Most fish can tolerate either fresh water or salt water, not both. Sturgeons, however, are unusual in that they are anadromous, meaning that they migrate from the sea to

European sturgeon habitats

fresh water to breed. Adult sturgeons spend most of the year in the deep oceans. Yet, as spring arrives, these fish feel the call of Nature and begin to return to the very rivers in which they were born. Swimming upstream, against the current, females lay their eggs over beds of gravel, which stick to the rocks and stones. The males spray the eggs with sperm, then both adults return to the ocean, leaving the young to hatch, unattended.

After the fry are born, they spend the first two years of their lives moving slowly downstream, feeding on insect

Comparisons

Sturgeons and paddlefish are closely related and share the same beaklike snout, although the latter lack the bony rows of scutes that are typical of sturgeon. American paddlefish (*Polyodon spathula*), like

their European relatives, are bottom feeders, cruising the Mississippi for plankton, which they strain from the water.

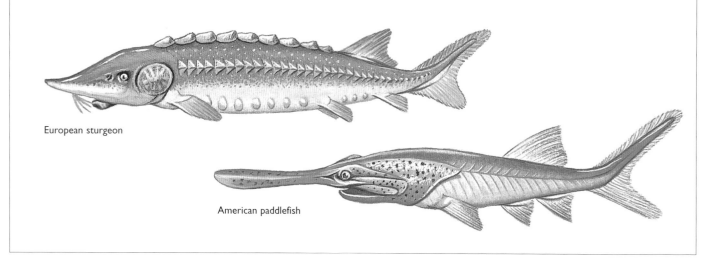

European sturgeon

American paddlefish

larvae until they are large enough to head out to sea. Sturgeon fry may be just 9cm (3.5in) long at birth, and grow to maturity slowly, eventually reaching up to 3m (9ft 10in) on an adult diet of invertebrates and fish.

It takes eight years before the sturgeon reaches sexual maturity and is ready to make the journey back from the ocean to the river in which it was spawned – a trip of up to 1000km (620 miles) for some species.

Threats and Conservation

Sturgeons may have been with us since the time of the dinosaurs, but these primitive fish unfortunately now face extinction worldwide. The most vulnerable are the star (*Acipenser stellatus*) and beluga sturgeon (*Huso huso*), which have been hunted since the time of the Romans for their meat and eggs. Female sturgeons can lay an amazing 34,000 eggs for every 1kg (2lb 3oz) of their body weight, and this roe, or caviar, is considered an expensive delicacy. Caviar from beluga sturgeon, for example, sells for US$100 an ounce (30g).

Since the break-up of the former Soviet Union, fish management has suffered and a growing illegal trade in Eurasian caviar has seriously depleted sturgeon numbers. In Europe, falling populations have been damaged further by the building of hydroelectric dams, which have destroyed traditional habitats and blocked routes to spawning grounds. Conservation efforts are already under way to save the sturgeon; however, as the fish can take 14 years to reach sexual maturity, progress in ensuring the sturgeon's future is both slow and uncertain.

Rooting in the silt and sand at the bottom of the ocean bed, the sturgeon uses its long snout to look for prey.

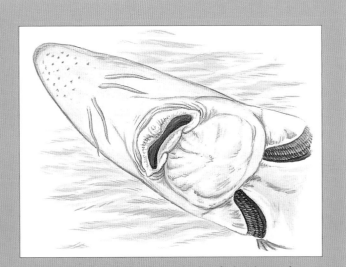

Long, bristly pairs of barbels are used to feel and taste for morsels of food in the gloomy ocean depths.

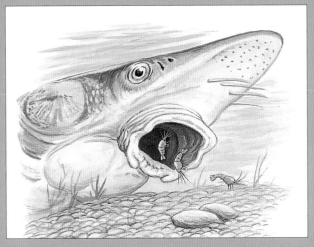

Most sturgeons, except the beluga, have downward-facing protrusile mouths, which thrust forwards to suck up food.

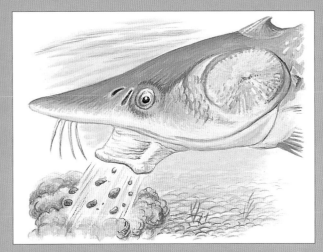

Edible food stuffs are swallowed, while mud and gravel are filtered out and spat back onto the seabed.

Great Bustard

Looking like a miniature ostrich, the great bustard is one of Europe's most unusual species. It had been hunted to extinction in the United Kingdom by 1832, and populations of this elegant bird are now vanishing at an alarming rate in other traditional strongholds such as Spain and Hungary.

Key Facts	ORDER *Gruiformes* / FAMILY *Otididae* / GENUS & SPECIES *Otis tarda*
Weight	Male 6–18kg (13–40lb); female 3.5–5.5kg (8–12lb)
Length	75–100cm (30in–39in)
Wingspan	1.9–2.6m (6ft 3in–8ft 6in)
Sexual maturity	Male 5–6 years; female 2–3 years
Breeding season	April–August
Number of eggs	1–4
Incubation period	21–28 days
Fledging period	30–35 days; independent at 80–120 days
Breeding period	1 year
Typical diet	Wide range of plant matter, insects and small vertebrates
Life span	Approximately 10–20 years

Wings

Huge wings are needed to keep these massive birds in the air. The wingspan of an adult male great bustard may measure as much as 2.1m (6ft 10in).

Foot
The Great Bustard has only
three large, broad toes.
Because it nests on the ground,
it has no need of a fourth hind
toe, which most birds use to
grip branches.

Great bustard habitats

The world's heaviest flying bird, the great bustard is a spectacular sight – instantly recognizable not just by its great size, but also by its spectacular plumage. Of the ten species of bustard listed on the IUCN's Red List, four of those, including the great bustard, are considered to be 'Endangered' or 'Vulnerable'.

What's in a Name?

Traditionally all animals have a Latin name that enables them to be clearly identified. In this system, called taxonomy, the great bustard's scientific name is *Otis tarda*. *Otis* is used to describe the bustard's dramatic throat feathers, while *tarda* means slow. Bustards are not especially slow-moving, but this is perhaps a reference to the way that they feed, grazing on seeds and grasses, and pausing between pecks, in a stately and deliberate way.

Common names – the names by which species are known locally – are often less easy to explain. Some names relate to legends and old tales. Others relate to the species' traits and attributes. No one knows for certain how this tall bird came to get such a curious English common name, but it is believed that 'bustard' comes from a corruption of the old French *bistarde*, or 'slow bird'.

All Change

The great bustard's natural habitats are grassland plains, an environment for which they are ideally camouflaged. At birth, chicks are grey in colour, with brown or black wavelike markings. At about two months, they begin to develop their adult plumage. Their necks remain grey, but their bodies change to a bold brown plumage, barred with black. Underneath they are white, with a red breast that becomes more prominent with age in males. It is during the mating season, though, that bustards undergo their

Comparisons

The red crested bustard (*Lophotis ruficrista*) shares many features with its larger, heavier cousin. It has long legs, a long neck and dramatically patterned plumage, which features cream, arrow-shaped bands. It also has an equally dramatic courtship display, performing a midair back flip while plummeting to the ground with its wings folded back.

Red-crested bustard

Great bustard

most dramatic costume change. Male bustards must compete for females with other males in a display arena known as a 'lek'. Here, males undergo a dramatic transformation, inflating their gular pouch and fanning out their feathers, which not only makes them appear bigger, but also changes their colour from brown to white. This balloon display is accompanied by vigorous stomping and soft 'umb umb' calls, which continue until the male finds a receptive female for mating.

Threats and Conservation

In the past, bustards were hunted to extinction in many parts of Europe, but today the biggest threat to their continued survival is intensive agriculture. Great bustards nest on the ground. Unfortunately, nesting often coincides with the ploughing season and, even if their eggs do survive intact, adult birds will generally abandon a nest when humans are near. In parts of Russia, farmers have started to leave islands of vegetation for the bustards, but predators have begun to recognize that these islands contain an unguarded food source. The solution has been to collect the eggs and use the chicks to reintroduce bustards to regions where they are now rare. Elsewhere, work to preserve the species is ongoing. The key is careful land management to ensure that this 'Vulnerable' species does not suffer a further fall in numbers.

Great bustard males reach sexual maturity at five years of age. Females mature much earlier, at three or four years.

On average, female great bustards outnumber males by two to one, so competition for a mate is fierce.

Displaying males inflate their neck sacs, fan out their tails and turn their wings over to reveal the feather's white underside.

It may take a few years of practice before the male's display becomes impressive enough to attract a mate.

Monk Seal

In Ancient Greece, fishermen considered monk seals to be an omen of good fortune. Sadly, their modern counterparts would much rather shoot these endearing mammals, believing that they poach 'their' fish stocks.

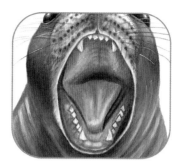

Teeth
Monk seals cannot chew their food because their teeth have no flat surfaces. Instead, these long, miniature daggers are used to pierce and tear flesh.

Pup

When monk seal pups are born, they have black, woolly coats, with distinctive white or yellow patches on their bellies. As they grow to adulthood, this soft fur is gradually replaced with a pale grey-brown coat. This may become totally black as an individual seal ages, although a white ventral (or chest) patch remains.

Key Facts	ORDER *Pinnipedia* / FAMILY *Phocidae* GENUS & SPECIES *Monachus monachus*
Weight	Male 170–260kg (375–573lb); Female 220–300kg (485–661lb)
Length	Male 2.1–2.6m (6ft 10in–8ft 6in); Female 2.3–2.7m (7ft 6in–8ft 10in)
Sexual maturity	5 years
Mating season Hawaiian monk seal Mediterranean monk seal	December–August; April–December
Gestation period	300–330 days
Number of young	1
Birth interval	2 years
Typical diet	Fish and cephalopods; sometimes crustaceans
Life span	Up to 30 years

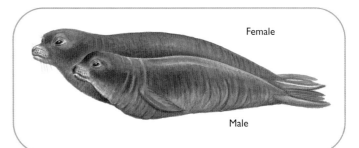

Female

Male

Size

Far larger than the male, the female monk seal can outweigh him by up to 100kg (220lb).

Monk seal habitats

Seals, sea lions and walruses belong to the order Pinnipedia. In Latin, *pinnipedia* means 'fin-footed', referring to the blunt, fin-shaped flippers that are characteristic of the species.

Fins, Feet and Flippers

The seal's flippers represent the first stage in the evolution of the pinnipeds from land mammals to an aquatic species. Seals have developed over millions of years so that their leg bones, above the ankle, are inside their body. This means that their flippers are really feet that have been adapted for use as paddles. And very effective they are, too, able to propel a seal through the water at top speeds of 16km/h (almost 10 mph).

In the case of the monk seal, the evolution from land to ocean dweller seems to have stopped short, as monk seals have both fur and nails and, because they are air breathers, they still need to come onto land to give birth. This means that their truncated legs still have a use, although limited. To get around on land, these shy and gentle mammals use their front legs, aided by lots of vigorous wriggling. The rear limbs are swept back and are little use for locomotion.

Secret Caves

Monk seals reach sexual maturity at around five years of age. Little is known about their courtship and mating, but females begin to arrive at birthing sites between September and November.

In the past, these sites would have included numerous sandy beaches throughout the Mediterranean; however, as these areas have become more popular with tourists, female seals have retreated to more secluded spots. Today's 'haul out' sites are more likely to be isolated cave systems, occasionally with underwater entrances. Here, seal mothers give birth to a single pup that weighs just 16kg (35lb). Fed by its mother's nutrient-rich milk, this newborn grows quickly. The month-long suckling period makes huge

Comparisons

Seals can be divided into two groups – true, or earless, seals (Phocidae) and eared seals (Otariidae). Both Baikal (*Phoca sibririca*) and monk seals are earless, with no obvious external ears. While monk seals prefer to bask in the warm waters of the Mediterranean, Baikals live in the chilly waters of Siberia's Lake Baikal.

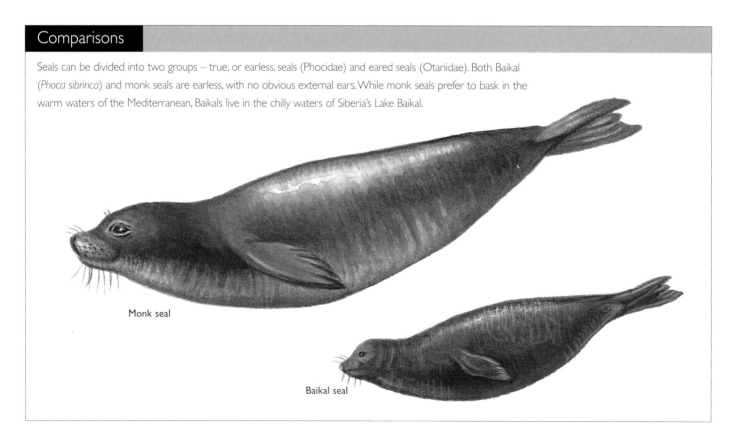

Monk seal

Baikal seal

physical demands on the mother, who may lose a third of her body weight before the pup is weaned. It may take up to two years before the juvenile pup leaves its mother's side completely, but during that time it will learn all the skills it needs to survive in the wild.

Threats and Conservation

The decline of the monk seal began during the time of the Roman Empire (31 BC–AD 476), when their fat was used extensively for lamp oil and their skin for clothing and shoes. Surviving colonies suffered another decline during the Middle Ages, and by the twenty-first century there were only scattered populations of monk seals left, in the Mediterranean, Ionian and Aegean seas, and off the north-west coast of Africa. In 1997, the largest of these colonies was virtually wiped out by a bloom of toxic algae, caused by pollution. Just two groups of monk seal are now considered viable, with enough individuals to sustain colony numbers.

The problems facing seal conservationists are difficult. In 1985, the French government initiated a captive breeding programme, but there were concerns about removing pups from populations that were already so beleaguered, and the programme was eventually abandoned. Despite legal protection throughout their range, seals also continue to suffer at the hands of fishermen, who see them as competition for their catch, and education initiatives are urgently needed to prevent this. With fewer than 500 monk seals left in the wild, extinction for these aquatic mammals may be just around the corner.

A monk seal takes a large gulp of air before diving to depths of 40m (131ft) in search of a meal.

Using its rear fins to control direction and to give thrust, the seal slips rapidly into the ocean depths.

A wide variety of marine animals is on the menu, but the favourite snack of Mediterranean and Hawaiian monk seals is octopus.

After a swift pursuit, the seal catches the octopus in its powerful jaws, then swims to the surface to enjoy its meal.

Red-breasted Goose

With rich chestnut brown plumage across their breast, neck
and the sides of the head, red-breasted geese are
one of the most attractive members of
the family Anatidae. Currently listed as
'Vulnerable', numbers of these
beautiful birds have fallen from
60,000 in 1970 to just
25,907 in 1990.

Feet
On land, red-breasted geese
walk with a distinct waddle,
but in water their large,
webbed feet make them
graceful swimmers.

Key Facts	ORDER *Anseriformes* / FAMILY *Anatidae* GENUS & SPECIES *Branta ruficollis*
Weight	2.5–3.5kg (5 lb 8oz–7lb 12oz)
Length	51–56cm (20–22in)
Wingspan	114–135cm (45–53in)
Sexual maturity	3–4 years
Breeding season	Summer; begins in June and chicks fledge by August
Number of eggs	3–7; usually 6 or 7
Incubation period	23–24 days
Fledging period	35–60 days
Breeding interval	Yearly
Typical diet	Leaves, stems, green grasses
Life span	Unknown

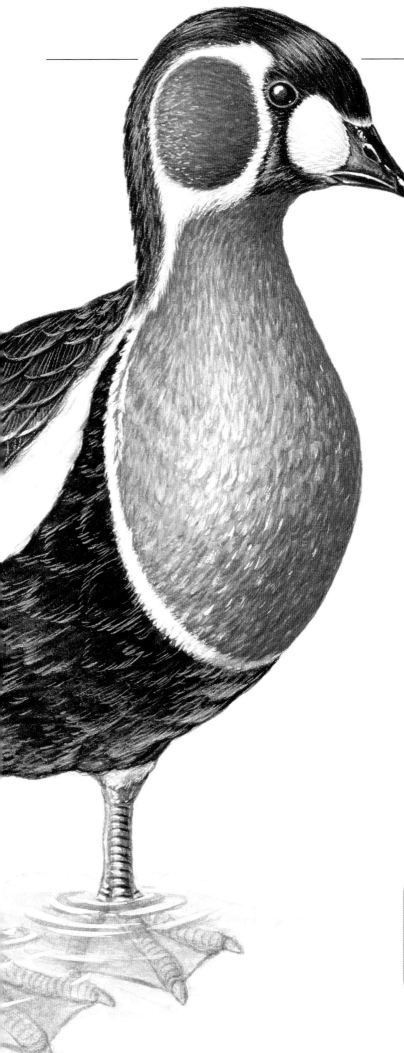

In flight
At the approach of winter, these beautiful geese make long migratory flights, overwintering in Bulgaria, Romania, the Ukraine and Greece, where conditions are more favourable. A distinctive 'kik-yoik, kik-yik' usually accompanies the flock as they fly by.

Bill
Red-breasted geese have a small bill with a fine serrated edge called 'lamellae'. This edge is used to cut up the grasses that form a major part of the geese's diet.

Red-breasted geese are known in Europe by a variety of names: *rothalsgans* in Germany, *bernache á cou roux* in France and *ganso de pecho rojo* in Spain.

Watering Holes

Red-breasted geese are vegetarian and can be found in habitats where there is a plentiful supply of winter wheat, barley, grasses and tubers. Water is an essential requirement, too. Geese, in common with other members of the family Anatidae, such as swans and ducks, spend much of their time in the water. Here, long tail feathers are a hazard, but the geese have short, stubby tails, which can be used like rudders to help them change direction when they swim. They are also able to make their plumage waterproof, using oily secretions from the uropygial gland, which is situated in the tail.

On land, geese are poor walkers because their feet are designed for swimming – set far back on the body, to help propel them through the water. For this reason, typical nest sites are in lichen-covered tundra and bush around lakes, rivers and reservoirs. This supplies the geese with fresh water for drinking and also with sand, which acts as a grinding mechanism to aid digestion.

Better the Devil You Know

In the winter, red-breasted geese migrate, flying to roosts on the Black Sea, in Bulgaria, Romania, the Ukraine and Greece, where the weather is warmer and the food more

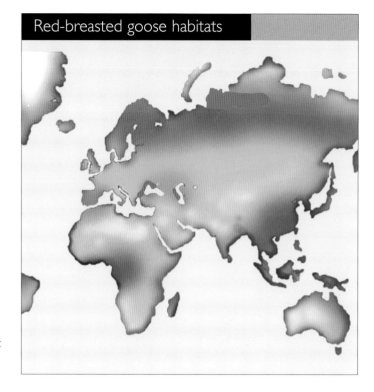

Red-breasted goose habitats

plentiful. In the summer, this unmistakable species returns to its ancestral breeding grounds in Russia's Yamal, Tainyr and Gydan peninsulas. Here, in early June, when the snow is beginning to melt, the geese begin their courtship displays, which are a way of rebonding with their mate for the season. Nests, lined with down and vegetation, are

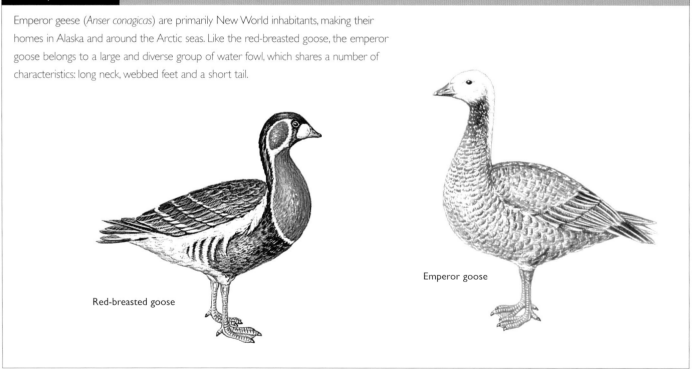

Comparisons

Emperor geese (*Anser conagicas*) are primarily New World inhabitants, making their homes in Alaska and around the Arctic seas. Like the red-breasted goose, the emperor goose belongs to a large and diverse group of water fowl, which shares a number of characteristics: long neck, webbed feet and a short tail.

Red-breasted goose

Emperor goose

built on steep riverbanks or craggy rock faces. Surprisingly, such sites are deliberately chosen because they are close to the nests of birds of prey such as peregrine falcons (*Falco peregrinas*) and snowy owls (*Nyctea scandiac*). Both species benefit from such a close association. The geese – who can be incredibly vocal when alarmed – keep the falcons alert to the presence of predators. And, in return, the falcons protect the geese from other hunters such as Arctic foxes (*Alopex lagopus*).

Threats and Conservation

Despite being listed as 'Vulnerable' by the IUCN, red-breasted geese are still hunted throughout their range, and in recent years there has been a sharp rise in the numbers of tourists travelling to Eastern Europe to shoot these appealing birds. The geese have also been affected by the decline in the population of peregrine falcons, which used to provide them with protection from predators. However, the greatest threat to their survival is habitat loss: 80–90 per cent of all red-breasted geese are confined to just five roost sites in Eastern Europe. If land use in these regions continues to change at its current rate, it is estimated that the geese will lose a further 67 per cent of their range by 2070. This is a disastrous prognosis for red-breasted geese, and coordinated work is needed to protect these striking birds throughout their migratory range

As conservationist Peter Scott (1909–1989) commented: 'Let us hope that the opportunity to fall in love with the beautiful red-breasted goose is affordable to others for many years to come.'

Red-breasted geese usually build their nests within 40m (131ft) of a large bird of prey, such as the rough-legged buzzard (*Buteo lagopus*).

Up to ten nesting pairs of geese take advantage of the buzzard's presence to nest, unmolested by other predators such as Arctic foxes.

Red-breasted chicks are nidifugous: they leave the nest very soon after hatching. (They can fly a month after they are born.)

With chicks of her own to feed, the buzzard can be a hazardous neighbour, so the goose chicks stay close.

Saiga

Able to run at speeds of up to 80km/h (50mph), and to scent out danger at vast distances, saigas have few natural enemies – apart from humans. They were once one of the great conservation success stories, but saiga numbers have fallen by 95 per cent in the past 20 years.

Hooves

Saigas walk on the middle two of their four toes. Cloven hooves such as this help the saiga to keep a grip on uneven ground.

Key Facts	ORDER *Artiodactyla* / FAMILY *Bovidae* GENUS & SPECIES *Saiga tatarica*	
Weight	25–70kg (55–154lb)	
Length Head and body Tail	1–1.4m (3ft 3in–4ft 6in) 6–12cm (2.4–4.7in)	
Shoulder height	60–80cm (24–31in)	
Sexual maturity	Female 10–12 months; males 19–20 months	
Mating season	December–January	
Gestation period	140–152 days	
Number of young	Usually 2, sometimes 1	
Birth interval	1 year	
Typical diet	Grasses, shrubs and herbs	
Life span	10–12 years	

Horns

Only male saigas grow horns. These are semi-translucent, with rings around the bottom two-thirds. Sharp tips make them formidable weapons during the seasonal rut.

Nose

Although female saigas are hornless, and slightly smaller than the males, both sexes have these distinctive, flexible noses.

This curious-looking ungulate has long been a problem for taxonomists. In the past, it was grouped with goats in the genus *Capra*. More recently, it has been categorized as both an antelope and a gazelle. Now it is usually placed in the subfamily Caprinae – the goat-antelopes.

Prominent Proboscises

Saigas share many characteristics with both goats and antelopes, but their extremely distinctive appearance makes it impossible to confuse them for anything else.

During the summer, these unique antelope have thin coats, comprised of a bristly outer layer and woolly under layer. As winter approaches, this grows longer and thicker, turning from buff to almost totally white. Although female Saigas are hornless, mature males grow almost vertical

horns. These are semi-translucent, with broad spiral bands covering the first two thirds of the horn. These may not be as impressive as those of other antelope, but they can grow up to 25cm (10in) long and are tipped by razor-sharp points, making them useful defensive weapons. Their most prominent feature is their huge, inflated nose. This strange appendage has a dual purpose, to filter out dust during the dry summer migration and to heat cold air before it reaches the lungs in the winter.

Mobile Homes

Saigas were once a familiar sight throughout Western Europe and into Eurasia. Today, these little antelopes make their homes primarily on the sweeping grasslands of the Russian steppe. This is a nomadic species, spending its life

At the start of the breeding season, males compete with each other to control harems of up to 15 females.

Males who survive the breeding season lead the exodus back to the herd's summer feeding grounds.

Females stay behind to give birth, and join the rest of the herd only once the calves are strong enough.

Newborns (usually twins) are able to graze after a few days, but continue to suckle from their mother for two months.

on the move. In the winter, large herds gather together for the long migrations south, towards fresh pastures in the warmer, sheltered mountain valleys. Here they spend the winter, feeding on a selection of shrubs, herbs and grasses. The 'rut' begins in November, when males begin to herd females into small harems to breed.

This is an intense time for males. Battles for breeding rights can be bloody and deadly, and 90 per cent of all males may die from sheer exhaustion by the time that the spring migration arrives. The survivors join the females and newborn calves on the long trek back to the steppes, which are blooming with vegetation at this time of year. A healthy herd can cover as many as 116km (72 miles) a day, even the newborn calves.

Threats and Conservation

In the old Soviet Union, Saigas were the subject of energetic conservation efforts, which saw them brought back from the brink of extinction to almost a million in number. Since the collapse of the Soviet Union, however, species management has suffered a huge setback. Habitat loss, road and canal construction, and poaching have all had a dramatic impact, and in just ten years saiga numbers have fallen to 50,000.

Due in part to the massive loss of males during the rut, there have always been more female than male saigas. Saigas live for only six to ten years, and the males do not reach sexual maturity until two years of age. This means

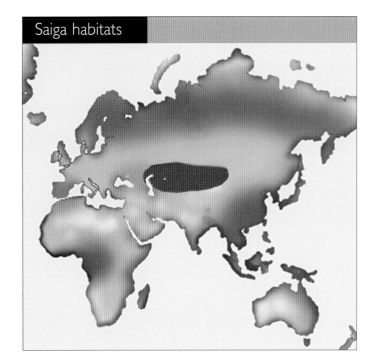

Saiga habitats

that the window of opportunity for successful mating is very narrow. As the male horns are valued in Chinese medicines, hunting has made this situation even more extreme. In some parts of their range, males are so rare that females have even been seen fighting over them. Increased protection, funding and the enforcement of existing anti-poaching laws are all urgently needed to protect what remains of this critically endangered species.

Comparisons

Saigas share part of their home range with the zeren (*Procapra gutturosa*). These Mongolian antelopes lack the distended nose that characterizes the saiga, but males do develop a similarly curious enlarged throat sac during the mating season. They also have short, dark grey, ringed horns – although these bend backwards, in a lyre shape.

Zeren

Saiga

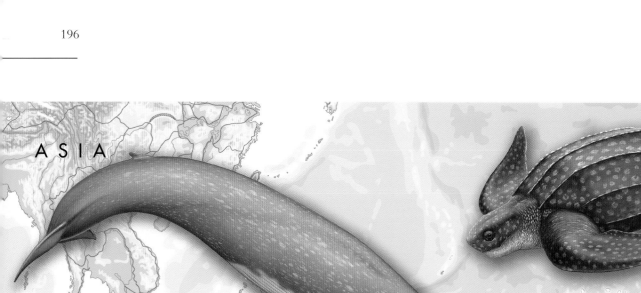

ASIA

PACIFIC
OCEAN

SOUTH
CHINA SEA

ARAFURA
SEA

TIMOR SEA

CORAL
SEA

INDIAN
OCEAN

AUSTRALIA

SOUTHERN
PACIFIC
OCEAN

SOUTH
AUSTRALIAN
BASIN

TASMAN
SEA

SOUTHERN
OCEAN

The World's Oceans

If we were to look at the Earth from space, we would see
a blue planet. From the icy waters of the Arctic to the tepid
tropical seas, water covers an amazing 70 per cent
of our home.

~

Cartographers classify the largest of these great oceans as the Pacific, which covers one-third of the world's entire surface. Next in size comes the Atlantic, then the Indian, which is the warmest of all the world's waterways. The babies of the family are the freezing Arctic and Antarctic oceans, which cover the Northern and Southern Hemisphere, respectively. For many of the inhabitants of this hidden world, such divisions are arbitrary. This is, in reality, one global ocean, and whether they are predators or herbivores, coastal or deep-sea dwellers, they all feel the harmful effects of pollution, overfishing and climate change which are responsible for the decline of certain species.

For centuries, the oceans have been indiscriminately used as the world's waste disposal unit. Toxic waste, sewage, agricultural runoff and oil spills are poisoning not only the ocean's inhabitants, but also ourselves, as these toxins find their way into the food chain. Commercial fishing and hunting has decimated populations of both fish and marine mammals such as whales. And the world's coral reefs with their unique ecosystems are slowly being killed by ever-rising global temperatures. The problems that face the ocean's wildlife are bigger than just how to save one species. Unless pollution and overfishing are checked, there is a very real possibility that the inhabitants of this last great frontier may vanish for ever.

Blue Whale

George F. Will, writing in the *Washington Post*, said, 'The campaign to save the whales is a rare and refreshing example of intelligence in the service of something other than self-interest.' Unfortunately, for the blue whale, this rare moment of clarity may have come too late.

Blowholes
Blue whales have twin blowholes, or 'spouts'. These are used to expel stale air when the whales surface from a dive.

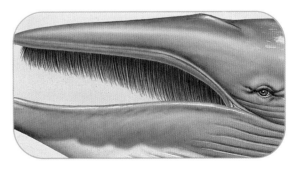

Baleen plates
Blue whales do not have teeth. Instead, a fringe of keratin hangs from their upper jaw. This is used to strain food from the water.

Tail

All whales have the same basic streamlined body shape as fish. The most obvious physical difference is their tails. Fish have vertical tail fins, but a whale's are horizontal.

Key Facts

ORDER *Cetacea* / FAMILY *Balaenopteridae* / GENUS & SPECIES *Balaenoptera musculus*

Weight	132 tons (146 tonnes)
Length	22–27m (72–88ft 6in) on average. The largest on record reached just over 33m (108ft)
Sexual maturity	5–10 years
Mating season	Midsummer in each hemisphere
Gestation period	11 months
Number of young	1
Birth interval	2–3 years
Typical diet	Krill
Life span	Not known, but estimated at up to 100 years

Blue whale habitats

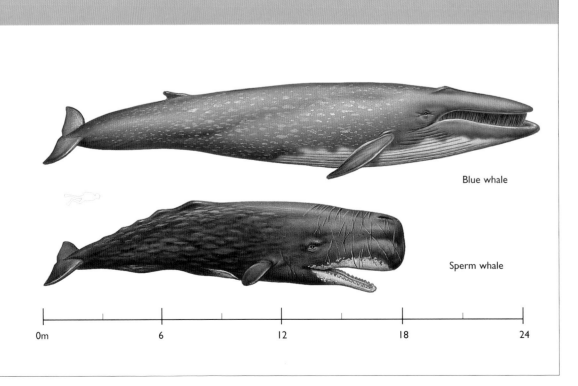

These huge, warm-blooded air-breathers belong to the family Balaenopteridae, members of which are also known as rorquals. Because of this, blue whales are also known as sulphur-bottom rorquals – in reference to their yellowish underbellies, which are caused by a type of algae called diatoms.

Feast and Fast

There are two distinct types of whales: those with teeth (the Odontoceti) and those without (the Mysticeti). Toothless whales, such as the blue whale, have no teeth, but rather huge mouths to accommodate a specialized feeding system called 'baleen plates'. Baleen plates are composed of a mass of hairs, which were once used to make 'whalebone' corsets. When not in use, these plates are covered by the whale's lower lip, which projects above the lower jaw. To feed, the whale simply opens its mouth, effectively filtering its food from the water.

Despite their vast size, blue whales are not hunter-killers like orcas (*Orcinus orca*). Instead, they feed on tiny shrimplike organisms called krill. During the summer, blue whale populations, from both the North and Southern hemispheres, migrate towards their respective poles to feed. An adult blue whale may consume 6 tonnes (5.4 tons) of krill a day, and over four months the whales become noticeably fatter. For the rest of the year, they eat nothing at all, surviving on the fat reserves built up during their summer feeding frenzy.

Big and Blue-tiful

There is only one word to describe a blue whale: gargantuan. This gentle marine mammal is the largest animal that has ever lived. As big as a Boeing 737, or 24 elephants, this creature is the Mount Everest of the animal kingdom. As David Day, in his book *The Whale War*, commented:

'*The heart of the Blue Whale is the height of a tall man and weighs half a ton. It beats like a huge kettle drum and its valves pump a sea of hot blood down its ... bulk, through arteries so big a child could crawl through them.... They are truly miraculous forms of life, which have been the largest-brained creatures on this planet thirty times longer than humans have existed at all.*'

Comparisons

Sperm whales – or 'cachalots', as they are known – are the largest of the toothed whales. They get their strange name from the oil, called spermaceti, which whalers took from their huge, square, bulbous heads. Even at 18m (59ft) long, sperm whales are tiny compared to the giant blue whales.

Blue whale

Sperm whale

0m   6   12   18   24

The blue whale's body is 30m (98ft) long, which represents a staggering 50 tonnes (45 tons) of muscle, 8 tonnes (7.25 tons) of blood and 60 tonnes (54 tons) of skin and bones. Sadly, for four hundred years, such statistics are all that these spectacular mammals have represented to humankind.

Threats and Conservation

Whales have been killed for their meat for thousands of years, but it was not until the 1600s that the Dutch and English began to hunt them in huge numbers. Within a hundred years, they had exhausted the whale 'supply' around Svalbard and moved on to other areas of the Arctic. By the 1800s, American whalers had joined the kill, developing the first 'factory ships', where the whales could

be rendered down into oil on board. This development meant that more whales could be hunted before the ship had to return to port, allowing some voyages to last up to five years. By the middle of the nineteenth century, the US whaling fleet alone killed 10,000 whales annually. Although whaling gradually declined in the United States, it continued to be a profitable business in Eastern Europe, and by the 1960s mechanization had increased the annual kill rate to 66,000.

In 1946, an International Whaling Commission was established to regulate the whaling business. It was hoped that temporary moratoriums and quotas would give whale populations a chance to re-establish themselves. Despite a total ban on blue whale hunting in 1966, species numbers have not recovered and this mammal still faces extinction.

Blue whales are solitary, generally feeding alone or in small family groups composed of a mother and her calves.

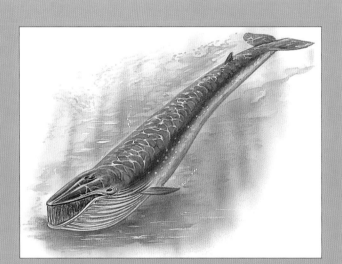

Most of the blue whale's food can be found at depths of less than 100m (328ft).

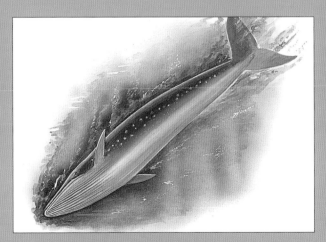

After a series of shallow dives, the whale makes a longer, deeper dive, headlong into the depths.

On the surface, the whale expels stale, hot breath. This hits the cold ocean air as a plume of condensation.

Dugong

For centuries, these slow sea cows were hunted for their meat, oil and bones. Today, populations of these gentle mammals have fallen to such low numbers that they are classified as a 'Vulnerable' species on the IUCN's Red List.

Key Facts	ORDER *Sirenia* / FAMILY *Dugongidae* / GENUS & SPECIES *Dugong dugon*
Weight	Up to 900kg (1984lb), but usually 230–360kg (507–794lb)
Length	2.5–4m (8ft 2in–13ft 1in)
Sexual maturity	9–10 years, but may be delayed until 15 years
Mating season	All year
Gestation period	13–14 months
Number of young	1; rarely, twins
Birth interval	3–7 years
Typical diet	Sea grasses; some seaweed
Life span	Up to 50 years

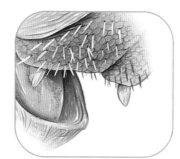

Mouth

At the tip of the dugong's bulbous head is a blunt snout and a pair of mobile, bristle-covered lips, which are used to pluck up bunches of aquatic vegetation. Projecting forward from the upper jaw is a pair of enlarged incisor teeth. These tusks are usually visible only in old age.

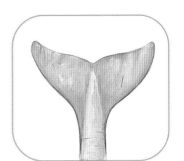

Tail
The dugong's T-shaped tail is this marine mammal's main method of propulsion.

Dugong habitats

At one time, sea cows were found throughout the world's warmer, tropical seas. The largest colonies can now be found around Northern Australia and New Guinea.

Sirens

It may be hard to believe, but these, bulbous, slate-grey mammals were probably the inspiration for the old sailor's stories about mermaids – the half-woman, half-fish spirits that seafarers have told tales about for centuries. In fact, the word 'dugong' comes from the Malay *duyung*, which means 'lady of the sea'.

Dugongs belong to the order Sirenia, a word that has its origins in 'siren'. In Greek mythology, the sirens were sea nymphs who attempted to lure ships onto the rocks with their irresistible songs. In Homer's famous tale *The Odyssey*, Odysseus manages to save his crew from the calls of the sirens by blocking their ears with wax. Odysseus had himself tied to the mast so that he could hear the siren's magical songs without endangering his ship. Dugongs may not be half-fish, half-woman, but they do make an eerie whistling call when danger is near.

There's No Hurry

Dugongs live their lives at a sedate pace. These gentle vegetarians spend much of their time in warm, shallow coastal waters. Here, they divide their day between feeding and resting. Sea grasses are the dugong's preferred food, which they suck up from the seabed using their flexible upper lips to tear up vegetation – roots and all. Adult Dugongs will slowly munch their way through around 100kg (220lb) of vegetation every day, making regular

Comparisons

There are two known families of sea cow: the manatees (Trichechidae) and the dugongs (Dugongidae). Manatees are only partially adapted to an aquatic life and still have hair on their bodies, nails on their flippers and a rounded, less efficient tail. Steller's sea cow (*Hydrodamalis stelleri*) once ranged throughout the North Pacific, but became extinct in 1768.

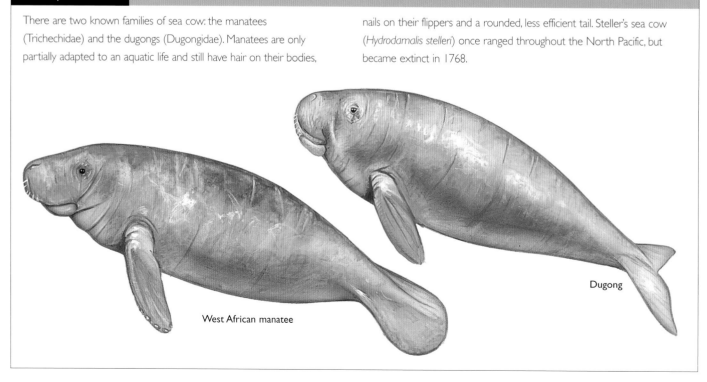

West African manatee

Dugong

dives to the seabed for food, before surfacing again for air. Dugongs can live up to 50 years of age, and much of their lives seem to be lived at the same sedate pace. Even breeding is an unhurried affair. Compared to other mammals, dugongs breed incredibly slowly. A single calf may be born every three to seven years. As dugongs reach sexual maturity only at nine or ten, a female may have fewer than five calves during her whole life.

Threats and Conservation

Dugongs are now legally protected from hunters who, for generations, have killed these 'sea sirens' for their meat and blubber, which were rendered down to make oil. Yet a wide range of other threats continues to contribute to their declining numbers. Despite being aquatic, dugongs still need to surface to breathe, and many are drowned each year when they become entangled in fishing nets. Pollution and silting have also depleted supplies of sea grass, which they rely on for food.

However, it is the dugong's slow rate of reproduction that explains why attempts to re-establish the species have been only moderately successful. Fortunately, these appealing mammals do have a high profile. In regions such as Australia, dugongs can enjoy the relative safety of habitats such as the Great Barrier Reef World Marine Park, and 16 other dugong protection areas. More research on their lifestyles is needed to ensure that conservation efforts are focused on the areas of greatest need, but luckily the world finally seems to be aware of the value of this real-life mermaid.

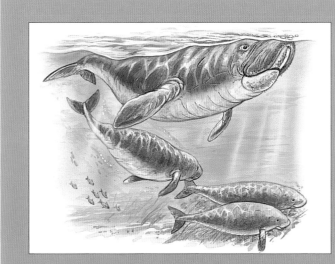

Bands of a few hundred dugongs have been spotted, but they generally live alone, or in small family groups.

Dugongs may be placid, but when in danger they are capable of spurts of speed of up to 25km/h (15.5mph).

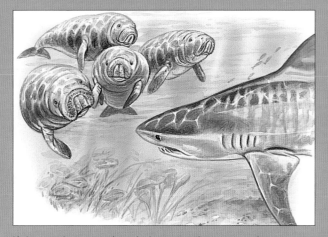

If danger threatens the whole group, dugongs are known to 'bunch up' in a defensive formation.

If that fails to deter the intruder, the dugongs will attempt to drive the intruder away with high-speed head-butts.

Great White Shark

Much of what we think we know about this immense fish is based on fiction, not fact. The great white shark's fearsome reputation may sell books and films, but it has done little to help this much-misunderstood rare fish in its fight for survival.

Teeth

A shark's teeth are like a bread knife – broad, sharp and with a jagged, serrated edge. These teeth grow in two rows, so that there is always a 'spare' ready to replace old, worn-out teeth.

A bigger bite

When prey is in sight, the great white lifts up its rounded snout. This brings its bottom jaw into line with its top – and so increases this hunter's bite capacity.

Key Facts	ORDER *Lamniformes* / FAMILY *Lamnidae* GENUS & SPECIES *Carcharodon carcharias*
Weight	600–1200kg (1320–2640lb)
Length	3.6–7.6m (12–25ft); female usually larger than male
Sexual maturity	About 7 years
Mating season	Varies with habitat
Gestation period	Probably about 12 months
Number of young	1 or 2
Birth interval	Unknown
Typical diet	Fish, squid, seals, dolphins, sea turtles, seabirds and whale carcasses
Life span	30–50 years

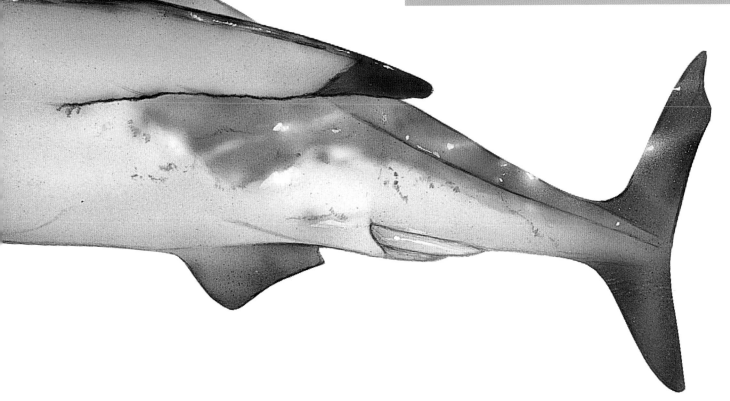

Shark habitats

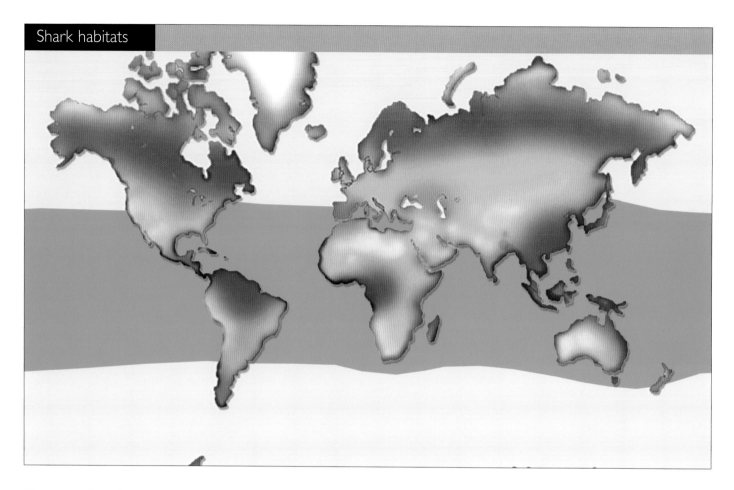

Known as the white pointer, the amaletz and the great white shark, this colossal member of the family Lamnidae may grow to 10m (32ft 10in) in length and more than 1.8 tonnes (1.6 tons) in weight.

Comparisons

Whale sharks (*Rhincodon typus*) may look dangerous, but these immense fishes are true gentle giants. Great white sharks are carnivores, but whale sharks feed on plankton – tiny plantlike organisms that they eat by straining sea water through their platelike teeth.

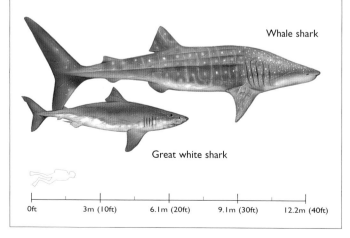

Whale shark

Great white shark

| 0ft | 3m (10ft) | 6.1m (20ft) | 9.1m (30ft) | 12.2m (40ft) |

A Little Nibble

Great white sharks are formidable hunters, but they are far from being the indiscriminate killers portrayed in fiction. All animals, with the exception of humans, hunt for food, not for fun. And sharks are no exception. Predators such as the great white sit at the very top of the food chain, and feed on a huge variety of prey. Favourite meals include seals, sea turtles, sea otters, squid and crabs. Occasionally other sharks are added to the menu.

The shark's greatest weapons are in its mouth. These sleek and fast marine dwellers are equipped with two rows of razor-sharp, wedge-shaped teeth, which are able to slice through flesh with ease. New teeth regularly replace the old, ensuring that the shark is always 'fully armed'. As sharks bite, they lift up their snouts. This pushes the bottom jaw into alignment with the top, giving them a huge bite capacity – 14kg (31lb) of food in a single mouthful. However, despite their reputation, sharks do not seem to deliberately hunt humans. They are dangerous, and they do kill people, but most attacks seem to be test bites, to determine the identity of an unfamiliar object.

Ancient Designs

Sharks belong to an ancient group of fish whose design is so successful that it has changed little in 400 million years.

Sharks have been called 'swimming noses', as their sense of smell is so sensitive that they can pick up the smallest chemical changes in the water, which tell them prey is near.

They can also detect the incredibly small electrical fields generated by the bodies of their prey. This allows them to home in on a meal, even in the gloomiest of waters.

Raising its snout just before it impacts with its prey allows the great white to bring its bottom jaw into line with its top one for a bigger bite.

This first bite is often a test. If the great white shark likes what it has tasted, then it will return to its victim to finish off the meal.

Unlike most fish, shark have a boneless skeleton, made up of an elastic substance called cartilage. They also lack the usual swim bladder (used by fish to keep afloat). Instead, sharks have an oil-rich liver to improve their buoyancy.

Despite these differences in design, sharks are agile and active. Great white sharks usually swim at quite a sedate pace, holding their bodies stiff and using their tails to provide the motion. This is an efficient and energy-saving technique that allows them to cruise for long periods of time. When possible prey is near, however, they are capable of sudden and dramatic spurts of speed, turning quickly to make unexpected attacks. They can even jump clear out of the water, in an amazing display of athleticism and acrobatics.

Threats and Conservation

It is impossible to say exactly how much harm films such as the 1975 blockbuster *Jaws* have done to the great white shark, as there are no accurate records of numbers. In fact, for a creature that has featured so prominently in popular culture, we know very little about its lifestyle at all. Currently this species is listed as 'Vulnerable' by the IUCN, but it is believed that numbers are so low that it may soon have to be reclassified as 'Endangered'. Until more is known, the biggest task facing conservationists is changing people's impressions of this fearsome fish, which many fisherman still view as the ultimate prize. In parts of South Africa and Southern Australia, this is already happening, as ecotourists flock to see these sharks in all their wild, natural glory.

Leatherback Turtle

The world's largest living turtles, leatherbacks have been listed as 'Endangered' since 1970. Now on the critical list, these remarkable reptiles have been brought to the brink of extinction by pollution, predation and poaching.

Key Facts	ORDER *Chelonia* / FAMILY *Dermochelyidae* GENUS & SPECIES *Dermochelyus coriacea*
Weight	300–500kg (660–1100lb)
Length	Up to 2.7m (8ft 10in)
Sexual maturity	When carapace reaches a span of 1.3–1.45m (4ft 3in–4ft 9in)
Nesting season	Dependent on location; almost any time of year
Number of eggs	Up to 900 each season. Laid in clutches of 80–90 eggs, at 10-day intervals.
Incubation period	55–74 days
Breeding interval	2–3 years
Typical diet	Jellyfish, crustaceans, molluscs
Life span	Up to 100 years or more

Hind flippers

The turtle's hind flippers are much shorter than its oversized fore flippers. These are used, like rudders, to change direction when swimming.

Fore flippers

The leatherback's fore flippers are almost half the length of the turtle's body. These are used primarily for swimming, but females also need these powerful limbs to pull themselves up onto the shore where they lay their eggs.

Beak

In place of teeth, the leatherback has a sharp beak, which it uses to slice up its favourite food – jellyfish.

Eyes

Large eyes are needed in the ocean depths to help gather as much light as possible.

Leatherback turtle habitats

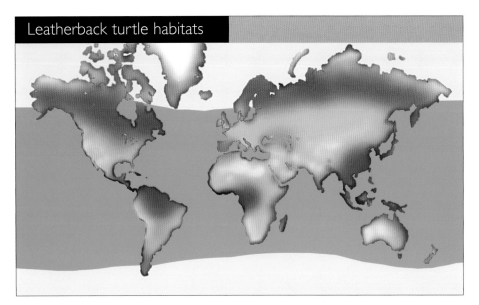

All turtles, tortoises and terrapins have a domed shell called a 'carapace'. In tortoises, these distinctive, high domes are made up of light to dark brown plates called 'scutes', which are fused to the axial skeleton (the bones comprising the skull and backbone). The leathery, or leatherback, turtle is unusual in that its carapace is not formed from fused vertebrae and ribs, but from soft connective tissue. The carapace joins the plastron (the lower shell) in a gentle curve, which gives their bodies a rounded appearance.

Tortoises, terrapins and turtles are reptiles. These diverse species are members of the cosmopolitan order Chelonia, which is distantly related to that of the lizard and snake.

Tortoises, Terrapins or Turtles?

The terms 'tortoise', 'terrapin' and 'turtle' are often used interchangeably, but in Britain terrestrial chelonians are usually considered to be tortoises. 'Terrapin' is the name generally given to freshwater aquatic species, while 'turtle' is the term used for chelonians that make their homes in the oceans.

The Cycle of Life

With their long fore flippers, designed for powering through the water, and short hind flippers that act as rudders, leatherback turtles are perfectly at home in the ocean. In fact, after they are born, male leatherbacks spend their entire lives at sea. Only the females ever venture onto land, revisiting the very beaches where they were born to lay their own eggs. This procedure can be torturous. While swift and agile in the water, turtles find movement difficult on land, and the females must pull themselves, inch by inch, up the beach, using their fore flippers as levers. Once the eggs have been laid, the turtles return to the water. Hatchlings emerge,

Comparisons

Leatherbacks have distinctive, heart-shaped carapaces, which are lined with seven longitudinal ridges. These look a little like tough brown leather – hence the name. Because of this, leatherbacks are often classified as the only member of the family Dermochelidae. Green turtles (*Chelonia mydas*) are more typical of other marine turtles, with their domed, horny carapaces.

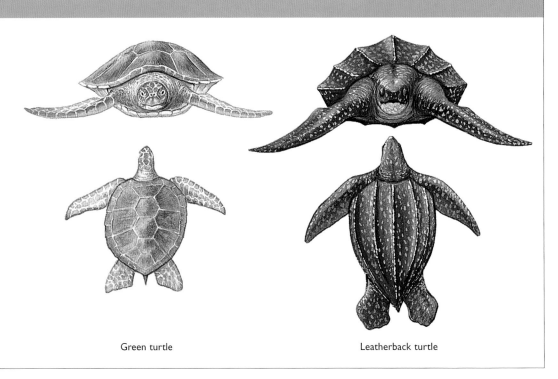

Green turtle

Leatherback turtle

unaided, around 60 days later. Digging their way up out of the sand towards freedom, these miniature turtles head for the ocean, and are generally not seen again until they reach maturity and they return to the beach (if they are female) for the whole cycle of life to begin again.

Threats and Conservation

Female turtles have the potential to lay 90 eggs, ten times a year, every three or four years for their entire adult lives. As turtles may live to be 100 years of age, that is a lot of eggs! In nature, this huge output is designed to compensate for the high mortality rate suffered by hatchlings. However, human activity has thrown the equation out of balance. Despite their protected status, eggs are still stolen from beaches, and females are often captured while nesting. Thousands of turtles are also killed accidentally every year – caught in fishing nets, poisoned by pollutants and attracted away from the beaches by car headlights, which the hatchlings mistake for the glow of the horizon. Plastic waste is a particular problem, as it is swallowed by turtles, who mistake it for their main prey, jellyfish. Scientists now estimate that only one in every 1000 leatherback hatchlings survive to adulthood.

In an attempt to combat the massive decline in leatherback numbers, the US government has recently banned longline fishing in areas of the Pacific. However, to ensure their secure future, international action is urgently needed to protect nesting sites from human activity.

Digging a hole in the soft sand, each female lays up to 90 eggs, around 70 of which are fertile. These nests are then covered with sand and left to incubate.

On a single night, all the eggs laid on the beach hatch at once. This gives the turtle hatchlings a better chance of surviving attacks by sea birds and reptiles.

Leatherback hatchlings that survive and reach the sea immediately begin to head for deeper waters. They may swim for 24 hours until they reach the safety of the ocean depths.

Leatherback turtles live a solitary existence in the world's oceans, but every three or four years adult females release chemical signals, called pheromones, to attract a mate.

Right Whale

In 1851, American author Herman Melville (1819–1891) immortalized the brutal world of the whaler in his novel *Moby Dick*. Today, it is hard to believe that an animal as spectacular as the right whale could have been hunted to near extinction simply to provide the raw materials for perfume, corsets, umbrellas and oil lamps.

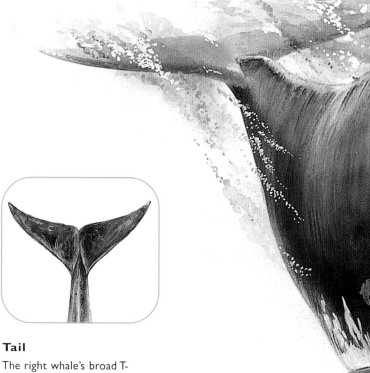

Key Facts	ORDER *Cetacea* / FAMILY *Balaenidae* GENUS & SPECIES *Eubalaena glacialis*	
Weight	30–80 tonnes (27–76 tons)	
Length	11–18m (36–59ft)	
Sexual maturity	7–12 years	
Mating season	Late winter, spring and early summer	
Gestation period	330–360 days	
Weaning period	4–8 months	
Breding interval	2–3 years	
Typical diet	Tiny marine animals: plankton, krill, small fish	
Life span	50–70 years	

Tail
The right whale's broad T-shaped tail is known as a 'fluke'. Unlike a fish's tail, flukes are horizontal, not vertical.

Blowhole

After a dive, the whale expels stale, hot breath. This hits the cold ocean air as a plume of condensation. Right whales are easy to spot because they have two blowholes, which produce a V-shaped plume.

Baleen plates

To feed, the whale simply opens its mouth. This allows the baleen plates, which hang down from the right whale's upper jaw like a huge net, to filter food from the water. When not in use, these plates are covered by the whale's lower lip, which projects above the upper jaw.

Callosities

Patches of tough, white skin grow around the whale's head. These 'callosities' are often infested with lice and can be used to help identify individual whales.

There are 11 known types of whale which feed using baleen plates in place of teeth – filtering their food through a thick fringe of a hairlike substance called keratin. These 'baleen' whales include grey whales, rorquals and right whales.

A Really Big Hug

Fish are cold-blooded, breathe through gills and usually lay eggs that are left to hatch unattended. Whales may look like fish, but they are mammals, which means that unlike fish they are warm-blooded, breathe air and give birth to live young and look after them. In fact, whales make very attentive parents.

These gentle giants reach sexual maturity at around ten years of age, when the male bulls and female cows begin to search for a mate. Whale courtship is often a playful affair, as the whales stroke each other with their flippers and (in the case of humpbacks) make energetic leaps from the water. Gestation takes around 12 months, after which a single calf is born in shallow coastal waters. Infants can weigh just under 1 ton (about 1 tonne) at birth and grow rapidly on a diet of nutritionally rich milk. During these vital early months, mother and baby are inseparable. Right whale mothers have even been seen to hug their calves, by rolling onto their bellies and embracing the baby in their flippers.

When Right Is Wrong

Toothless whales belong to the suborder Mysticeti, which means 'moustached'. This refers to the fringe of baleen, which becomes visible when the whales open their

A North Atlantic right whale surfaces from a dive, sending a jet of V-shaped condensation into the air.

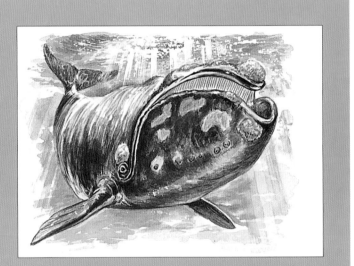

The right whale's food of choice is small, shrimplike krill, which can be found just beneath the surface.

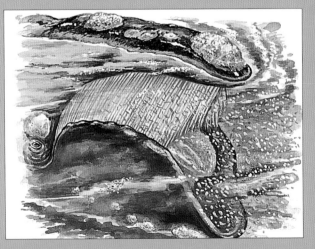

Opening its mouth to feed, the whale 'sucks in' water, using its baleen plates to filter out the krill.

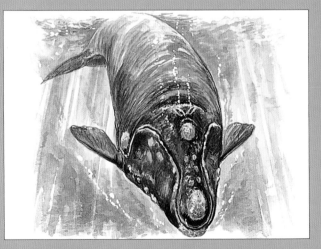

The trapped krill are swept up by the whale's tongue, as excess water is expelled through the baleen plates.

mouths to feed. Of the three types of baleen whales, the right whales are perhaps the most distinctive in appearance. Their bodies are thick and black in colour, with prominent patches of rough skin. These patches, or callosities, are usually covered in whale lice and can appear yellow in colour.

North Atlantic right whales have unusually large heads, which make up almost a quarter of the mammal's entire body. Here are found the most valuable oils and baleen (which was once used to make 'whalebone' corsets). And it is the head that was the reason these huge marine dwellers were considered to be the 'right' whales to hunt. These whales are also slow swimmers, with a characteristic V-shaped plume, a feature which made them easy pickings for whaling ships in the twentieth century.

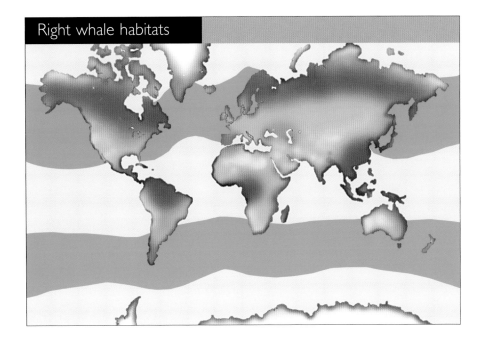

Right whale habitats

Threats and Conservation

Although right whales have been legally protected since 1935, centuries of exploitation have taken their toll. While today's populations are safe from hunters, the small remaining colonies are still declining. Right whales give birth in the shallows, and mothers will remain there until their young have been weaned. Here, they risk being hit by ships and drowned in fishing nets. It is estimated that a third of all right whale deaths are caused by such encounters. To combat this, moves have been made to redesign fishing gear and set aside protected, ship-free, habitats such as Cape Cod Bay and the Great South Channel, off the south-eastern United States. With a North Atlantic population of just 300–350 individuals, such moves are well intentioned, but may be too little, too late.

Comparisons

The North Atlantic right whale is almost the same size as the Greenland right, or bowhead, whale (*Balaena mysticetus*). Greenland right whales have even larger heads than their North Atlantic relatives; the head is one-third of this giant's entire body. For this reason, it, too, was extensively hunted and, although small numbers are still found in the Arctic waters, it is now extremely rare.

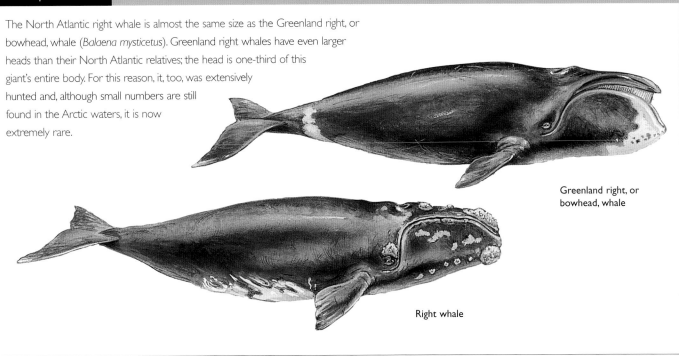

Greenland right, or bowhead, whale

Right whale

Sea Otter

It is estimated that populations of sea otter have fallen by as much as 90 per cent in the past few years. As a result, this lithe, athletic and appealing marine mammal is now on the world's growing list of 'Endangered' species.

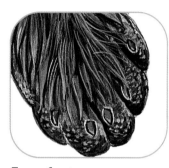

Fore feet

The sea otter's huge feet have five clawed toes. On the fore feet, these are retractable, which allows the otters to better manipulate their food.

Hind feet

Hind feet are larger than the fore feet and fully webbed to the tips of the toes. This provides greater propulsion when the otter swims.

Key Facts	ORDER *Carnivora* / FAMILY *Mustelidae* GENUS & SPECIES *Enhydra lutris*	
Weight	Male 22–45kg (49–99lb); Female 15–32kg (33–71lb)	
Length Head and body Tail	55–140cm (22–55in) 25–37cm (10–14.5in)	
Sexual maturity	Male 5 years; female 3 years	
Mating season	All year round, but peaks vary according to location	
Gestation period	Usually around 130 days; a further 240–350 days if implantation is delayed	
Number of young	1	
Birth interval	1 year	
Typical diet	Sea urchins, molluscs, crabs, octopus, fish	
Life span	15–20 years	

Teeth

Unusually for carnivores, sea otters have very few sharp cutting teeth (incisors). Instead, they have compact, rounded molars, which are used to crush the tough outer shells of molluscs.

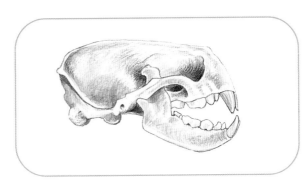

Sea otter habitats

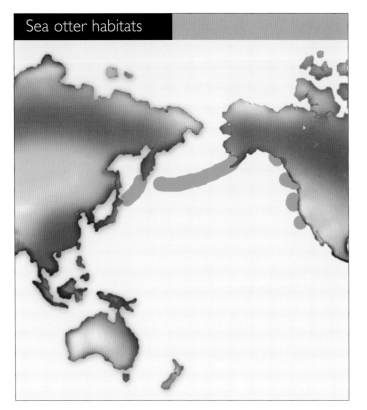

Sea otters are a 'keystone' species: their presence is vital to the health of regions such as North America's aquatic kelp forests. Here, these appealing mammals act as caretakers, preventing a build-up of sea urchins, which would otherwise decimate the vegetation.

All at Sea

Sea otters have the distinction of being the heaviest of all otters, but the smallest marine mammal. Unlike other otters, these long, streamlined members of the family Mustelidae spend almost their entire lives in the water. It is here that they hunt, feed, rest and mate.

Unusually for a marine mammal, sea otters do not have a thick insulating layer of blubber to keep them warm. Instead, they rely on their dense brown fur, which contains natural waterproofing oils. Nevertheless, they still need to consume at least 25 per cent of their body weight in shellfish, sea urchins and abalone every day in order to stay warm. Meals are usually eaten while the otter floats on its back, using its stomach as a table. Their fore feet are incredibly dexterous, but any shellfish that cannot be prised open manually is usually broken apart using a stone – a rare example of mammalian tool use. After a meal, a nap may be in order, and otters will often wrap themselves up in kelp beds to stop themselves drifting while resting.

Families and Friends

Sea otters are a gregarious species. Although it is rare for otters to hunt in packs, they seem to enjoy company and gather together in large, single-sex groups known as 'rafts' when resting. Depending on their location, these groups can number anything from 12 to 2000 individuals, who keep in constant contact with each other through a wide range of complex whines and squeals.

Comparisons

If sea otters are the largest members of the family, then the oriental small-clawed otter of Southeast Asia (Aonyx cinerea) is probably one of the smallest. At almost an eighth of the size of the sea otter, this small mustelid shares its cousin's reddish brown coloration, with paler fur covering the neck and much of the chest.

Oriental small-clawed otter

Sea otter

Between May and June in the north, and January and March in the south, these single-sex groups will begin to break up, as males and females start looking for a mate. Sea otters are polygamous, and males may mate with several females during the breeding season. Courtship is a playful affair, culminating in the birth of a single pup, which the mother teaches how to hunt and groom over an intense period of five months.

Threats and Conservation

Sea otter's coats are incredibly soft and thick, comprising around 150,000 hairs per square centimetre (0.15 square inch). This has made the species a popular target for hunters over the centuries. Today, new threats continue to threaten their survival. For instance, marine mammals need to surface to breathe, and are often killed accidentally when they drown after becoming entangled in fishing nets. Gill nets, which are used to catch salmon, are a particular problem for otters in the north, although laws have now prohibited their use in the shallows, where the sea otters gather.

Sea otters are also particularly vulnerable to pollution. In 1989, 2650 sea otters died after the *Exxon Valdez* oil spill in Alaska, and many scientists believe that, even all these years later, the region has not fully recovered. Arguments still rage over the future of this attractive mustelid, as commercial pressure from fishermen is high to remove their protected status along much of its range.

Relaxing after a meal, the otter wraps itself in a bed of sea kelp to stop itself from drifting with the tide.

Sea otters usually hunt in the shallow waters, at depths of 30m (98ft 5in), although they can manage double that.

Sea otters are skilled tool users, dislodging shellfish from the seabed with the aid of a carefully chosen rock.

A pouch of skin under the front flipper keeps the catch safe until it can be broken open and eaten on the surface.

Index